4th Workshop on Computational Approaches to Code Switching (CALCS 2020)

Marseille, France
11 – 16 May 2020

Editors:

Thamar Solorio
Monojit Choudhury
Kalika Bali

Sunayana Sitaram
Amitava Das
Mona Diab

ISBN: 978-1-7138-1258-6

LREC 2020 Workshop
Language Resources and Evaluation Conference
11–16 May 2020

4th Workshop on
Computational Approaches to Code Switching

PROCEEDINGS

Thamar Solorio, Monojit Choudhury, Kalika Bali, Sunayana Sitaram,
Amitava Das, and Mona Diab (eds.)

Proceedings of the LREC 2020
4th Workshop on ComputationalApproaches to Code Switching

Edited by: Thamar Solorio, Monojit Choudhury, Kalika Bali, Sunayana Sitaram, Amitava Das, and Mona Diab

For more information:
European Language Resources Association (ELRA)
9 rue des Cordelières
75013, Paris
France
http://www.elra.info
Email: lrec@elda.org

Preface

Welcome to the proceedings of the 4th workshop on Computational Approaches to Linguistic Code Switching (CALCS). Code-switching (CS) is the phenomenon by which multilingual speakers switch back and forth between their common languages in written or spoken communication. CS is pervasive in informal text communications such as news groups, tweets, blogs, and other social media of multilingual communities. Such genres are increasingly being studied as rich sources of social, commercial and political information. Moreover, CS language data is penetrating more traditional formal genres such as newswire in multilingual communities. Apart from the informal genre challenge associated with such data within a single language processing scenario, the CS phenomenon adds another significant layer of complexity to the processing of the data. Efficiently and robustly processing CS data still presents a new frontier for NLP algorithms on all levels. CS accordingly has been garnering more importance and attention both in academic circles, research labs, and industry. Furthermore, the current pandemic and associated guidelines of physical distancing has created a significant spike in online platform usage in an unprecedented manner. The usage is for social connectivity but even more relevant is for information seeking. This increase in social media usage translates to more CS language usage leading to an even more urgent need for processing.

The goal of this workshop is to bring together researchers interested in exploring these new frontiers, discussing state of the art research in CS, and identifying the next steps in this fascinating research area. The workshop program includes exciting papers discussing new approaches for CS data and the development of linguistic resources needed to process and study CS.

We received 14 submissions, 9 of which were accepted. The papers run the gamut from creation of novel resources (such as a corpus of Spanish newspaper headlines annotated for Anglicisms, to a conversational data set annotated for CS) to modeling papers exploring advanced models (such as multi-task learning for low resource languages, impact of script mixing on modeling, impact of word embeddings on Indonesian-English, multimodal modeling of acoustic and linguistic features for English-IsiZulu, parsing for CS data, efficient grapheme to phoneme conversion) to papers addressing applications such as sentiment analysis and acoustic modeling for speech recognition. Finally, the range of papers cover some novel languages not addressed in previous CALCS workshops such as Indonesian-English, Korean Transliteration, English IsiZulu, Algerian Arabic which code switches with Modern Standard Arabic and French. We would like to thank all authors who submitted their contributions to this workshop. We also thank the program committee members for their help in providing meaningful reviews. Lastly, we thank the LREC 2020 organizers for the opportunity to put together this workshop. See you online/virtually at LREC 2020!

Workshop Organizers
Thamar Solorio, University of Houston (USA)
Monojit Choudhury, Microsoft Research (India)
Kalika Bali, Microsoft Research (India)
Sunayana Sitaram, Microsoft Research (India)
Amitava Das, Wipro AI (India)
Mona Diab, Facebook AI, George Washington University (USA)

Organizers:

Thamar Solorio, University of Houston (USA)
Monojit Choudhury, Microsoft Research (India)
Kalika Bali, Microsoft Research (India)
Sunayana Sitaram, Microsoft Research (India)
Amitava Das, Wipro AI (India)
Mona Diab, Facebook AI, George Washington University (USA)

Program Committee:

Gustavo Aguilar, University of Houston
Barbara Bullock, University of Texas at Austin
Özlem Cetinoglu, University of Stuttgart
Hila Gonen, Bar Ilan University
Sandipan Dandapat, Microsoft
A. Seza Doğruöz, Independent Researcher
William H. Hsu, Kansas State University
Constantine Lingos, Brandeis University
Rupesh Mehta, Microsoft
Joel Moniz, Carnegie Mellon University
Adithya Pratapa, Carnegie Mellon University
Yihong Theis, Kansas State University
Jacqueline Toribio, University of Texas at Austin
Gentra Inda Winata, Hong Kong University of Science and Technology
Dan Garrett, Google

Table of Contents

An Annotated Corpus of Emerging Anglicisms in Spanish Newspaper Headlines
Elena Alvarez-Mellado 1

A New Dataset for Natural Language Inference from Code-mixed Conversations
Simran Khanuja, Sandipan Dandapat, Sunayana Sitaram and Monojit Choudhury 9

When is Multi-task Learning Beneficial for Low-Resource Noisy Code-switched User-generated Algerian Texts?
Wafia Adouane and Jean-Philippe Bernardy 17

Evaluating Word Embeddings for Indonesian–English Code-Mixed Text Based on Synthetic Data
Arra'Di Nur Rizal and Sara Stymne 26

Understanding Script-Mixing: A Case Study of Hindi-English Bilingual Twitter Users
Abhishek Srivastava, Kalika Bali and Monojit Choudhury 36

Sentiment Analysis for Hinglish Code-mixed Tweets by means of Cross-lingual Word Embeddings
Pranaydeep Singh and Els Lefever 45

Semi-supervised acoustic and language model training for English-isiZulu code-switched speech recognition
Astik Biswas, Febe De Wet, Ewald Van der westhuizen and Thomas Niesler 52

Code-mixed parse trees and how to find them
Anirudh Srinivasan, Sandipan Dandapat and Monojit Choudhury 57

Towards an Efficient Code-Mixed Grapheme-to-Phoneme Conversion in an Agglutinative Language: A Case Study on To-Korean Transliteration
Won Ik Cho, Seok Min Kim and Nam Soo Kim 65

Proceedings of the LREC 2020 – 4th Workshop on Computational Approaches to Code Switching, pages 1–8
Language Resources and Evaluation Conference (LREC 2020), Marseille, 11–16 May 2020
European Language Resources Association (ELRA), licensed under CC-BY-NC

An Annotated Corpus of Emerging Anglicisms in Spanish Newspaper Headlines

Elena Álvarez-Mellado

Department of Computer Science, Brandeis University
415 South St, Waltham, MA 02453
ealvarezmellado@brandeis.edu

Abstract

The extraction of anglicisms (lexical borrowings from English) is relevant both for lexicographic purposes and for NLP downstream tasks. We introduce a corpus of European Spanish newspaper headlines annotated with anglicisms and a baseline model for anglicism extraction. In this paper we present: (1) a corpus of 21,570 newspaper headlines written in European Spanish annotated with emergent anglicisms and (2) a conditional random field baseline model with handcrafted features for anglicism extraction. We present the newspaper headlines corpus, describe the annotation tagset and guidelines and introduce a CRF model that can serve as baseline for the task of detecting anglicisms. The presented work is a first step towards the creation of an anglicism extractor for Spanish newswire.

Keywords: borrowing extraction, anglicism, newspaper corpus

1. Introduction

The study of English influence in the Spanish language has been a hot topic in Hispanic linguistics for decades, particularly concerning lexical borrowing or anglicisms (Gómez Capuz, 2004; Lorenzo, 1996; Medina López, 1998; Menéndez et al., 2003; Núñez Nogueroles, 2017a; Pratt, 1980; Rodríguez González, 1999).

Lexical borrowing is a phenomenon that affects all languages and constitutes a productive mechanism for word-formation, especially in the press. Chesley and Baayen (2010) estimated that a reader of French newspapers encountered a new lexical borrowing for every 1,000 words. In Chilean newspapers, lexical borrowings account for approximately 30% of neologisms, 80% of those corresponding to English loanwords (Gerding et al., 2014).

Detecting lexical borrowings is relevant both for lexicographic purposes and for NLP downstream tasks (Alex et al., 2007; Tsvetkov and Dyer, 2016). However, strategies to track and register lexical borrowings have traditionally relied on manual review of corpora.

In this paper we present: (1) a corpus of newspaper headlines in European Spanish annotated with emerging anglicisms and (2) a CRF baseline model for anglicism automatic extraction in Spanish newswire.

2. Related Work

Corpus-based studies of English borrowings in Spanish media have traditionally relied on manual evaluation of either previously compiled general corpora such as CREA[1] (Balteiro, 2011; Núñez Nogueroles, 2016; Núñez Nogueroles, 2018b; Oncíns Martínez, 2012), either new tailor-made corpora designed to analyze specific genres, varieties or phenomena (De la Cruz Cabanillas and Martínez, 2012; Diéguez, 2004; Gerding Salas et al., 2018; Núñez Nogueroles, 2017b; Patzelt, 2011; Rodríguez Medina, 2002; Vélez Barreiro, 2003).

In terms of automatic detection of anglicisms, previous approaches in different languages have mostly depended on

resource lookup (lexicon or corpus frequencies), character n-grams and pattern matching. Alex (2008b) combined lexicon lookup and a search engine module that used the web as a corpus to detect English inclusions in a corpus of German texts and compared her results with a maxent Markov model. Furiassi and Hofland (2007) explored corpora lookup and character n-grams to extract false anglicisms from a corpus of Italian newspapers. Andersen (2012) used dictionary lookup, regular expressions and lexicon-derived frequencies of character n-grams to detect anglicism candidates in the Norwegian Newspaper Corpus (NNC) (Hofland, 2000), while Losnegaard and Lyse (2012) explored a Machine Learning approach to anglicism detection in Norwegian by using TiMBL (Tilburg Memory-Based Learner, an implementation of a k-nearest neighbor classifier) with character trigrams as features. Garley and Hockenmaier (2012) trained a maxent classifier with character n-gram and morphological features to identify anglicisms in German online communities.

In Spanish, Serigos (2017a) extracted anglicisms from a corpus of Argentinian newspapers by combining dictionary lookup (aided by TreeTagger and the NLTK lemmatizer) with automatic filtering of capitalized words and manual inspection. In Serigos (2017b), a character n-gram module was added to estimate the probabilities of a word being English or Spanish. Moreno Fernández and Moreno Sandoval (2018) used different pattern-matching filters and lexicon lookup to extract anglicism cadidates from a corpus of tweets in US Spanish.

Work within the code-switching community has also dealt with language identification on multilingual corpora. Due to the nature of code-switching, these models have primarily focused on oral copora and social media datasets (Aguilar et al., 2018; Molina et al., 2016; Solorio et al., 2014). In the last shared task of language identification in code-switched data (Molina et al., 2016), approaches to English-Spanish included CRFs models (Al-Badrashiny and Diab, 2016; Shrestha, 2016; Sikdar and Gambäck, 2016; Xia, 2016), logistic regression (Shirvani et al., 2016) and LSTMs models (Jaech et al., 2016; Samih et al., 2016).

---

[1]http://corpus.rae.es/creanet.html

The scope and nature of lexical borrowing is, however, somewhat different to that of code-switching. In fact, applying code-switching models to lexical borrowing detection has previously proved to be unsuccessful, as they tend to overestimate the number of anglicisms (Serigos, 2017b). In the next section we address the differences between both phenomena and set the scope of this project.

3. Anglicism: Scope of the Phenomenon

Linguistic borrowing can be defined as the transference of linguistic elements between two languages. Borrowing and code-switching have frequently been described as a continuum (Clyne et al., 2003), with a fuzzy frontier between the two. As a result, a precise definition of what borrowing is remains elusive (Gómez Capuz, 1997) and some authors prefer to talk about code-mixing in general (Alex, 2008a) or "lone other-language incorporations" (Poplack and Dion, 2012).

Lexical borrowing in particular involves the incorporation of single lexical units from one language into another language and is usually accompanied by morphological and phonological modification to conform with the patterns of the recipient language (Onysko, 2007; Poplack et al., 1988). By definition, code-switches are not integrated into a recipient language, unlike established loanwords (Poplack, 2012). While code-switches are usually fluent multiword interferences that normally comply with grammatical restrictions in both languages and that are produced by bilingual speakers in bilingual discourses, lexical borrowings are words used by monolingual individuals that eventually become lexicalized and assimilated as part of the recipient language lexicon until the knowledge of "foreign" origin disappears (Lipski, 2005).

In terms of approaching the problem, automatic code-switching identification has been framed as a sequence modeling problem where every token receives a language ID label (as in a POS-tagging task). Borrowing detection, on the other hand, while it can also be transformed into a sequence labeling problem, is an extraction task, where only certain spans of texts will be labeled (in the fashion of a NER task).

Various typologies have been proposed that aim to classify borrowings according to different criteria, both with a cross-linguistic perspective and also specifically aimed to characterize English inclusions in Spanish (Gómez Capuz, 1997, Haspelmath, 2008; Núñez Nogueroles, 2018a; Pratt, 1980). In this work, we will be focusing on unassimilated lexical borrowings (sometimes called *foreignisms*), i.e. words from English origin that are introduced into Spanish without any morphological or orthographic adaptation.

4. Corpus description and annotation

4.1. Corpus description

In this subsection we describe the characteristics of the corpus. We first introduce the main corpus, with the usual train/development/test split that was used to train, tune and evaluate the model. We then present an additional test set that was designed to assess the performance of the model on more naturalistic data.

4.1.1. Main Corpus

The main corpus consists of a collection of monolingual newspaper headlines written in European Spanish. The corpus contains 16,553 headlines, which amounts to 244,114 tokens. Out of those 16,553 headlines, 1,109 contain at least one anglicism. The total number of anglicisms is 1,176 (most of them are a single word, although some of them were multiword expressions). The corpus was divided into training, development and test set. The proportions of headlines, tokens and anglicisms in each corpus split can be found in Table 1.

The headlines in this corpus come from the Spanish newspaper *eldiario.es*[2], a progressive online newspaper based in Spain. *eldiario.es* is one of the main national newspapers from Spain and, to the best of our knowledge, the only one that publishes its content under a Creative Commons license, which made it ideal for making the corpus publicly available[3].

Set	Headlines	Tokens	Headlines with anglicisms	Anglicisms	Other borrowings
Train	10,513	154,632	709	747	40
Dev	3,020	44,758	200	219	14
Test	3,020	44,724	202	212	13
Suppl. test	5,017	81,551	122	126	35

Table 1: Number of headlines, tokens and anglicisms per corpus subset.

The headlines were extracted from the newspaper website through web scraping and range from September 2012 to January 2020. Only the following sections were included: economy, technology, lifestyle, music, TV and opinion. These sections were chosen as they were the most likely to contain anglicisms. The proportion of headlines with anglicisms per section can be found in Table 2.

Section	Percentage of anglicisms
Opinion	2.54%
Economy	3.70%
Lifestyle	6.48%
TV	8.83%
Music	9.25%
Technology	15.37%

Table 2: Percentage of headlines with anglicisms per section.

Using headlines (instead of full articles) was beneficial for several reasons. First of all, annotating a headline is faster and easier than annotating a full article; this helps ensure that a wider variety of topics will be covered in the corpus. Secondly, anglicisms are abundant in headlines, because they are frequently used as a way of calling the attention of the reader (Furiassi and Hofland, 2007). Finally, borrowings that make it to the headline are likely to be particularly salient or relevant, and therefore are good candidates for being extracted and tracked.

---

[2] http://www.eldiario.es/

[3] Both the corpus and the baseline model (Section 5) can be found at https://github.com/lirondos/lazaro.

4.1.2. Supplemental Test Set

In addition to the usual train/development/test split we have just presented, a supplemental test set of 5,017 headlines was collected. The headlines included in this additional test set also belong to *eldiario.es*. These headlines were retrieved daily through RSS during February 2020 and included all sections from the newspaper. The headlines in the supplemental corpus therefore do not overlap in time with the main corpus and include more sections. The number of headlines, tokens and anglicisms in the supplemental test set can be found in Table 1.

The motivation behind this supplemental test set is to assess the model performance on more naturalistic data, as the headlines in the supplemental corpus (1) belong to the future of the main corpus and (2) come from a less borrowing-dense sample. This supplemental test set better mimics the real scenario that an actual anglicism extractor would face and can be used to assess how well the model generalizes to detect anglicisms in any section of the daily news, which is ultimately the aim of this project.

4.2. Annotation guidelines

The term *anglicism* covers a wide range of linguistic phenomena. Following the typology proposed by Gómez Capuz (1997), we focused on direct, unadapted, emerging Anglicisms, i.e. lexical borrowings from the English language into Spanish that have recently been imported and that have still not been assimilated into Spanish. Other phenomena such as semantic calques, syntactic anglicisms, acronyms and proper names were considered beyond the scope of this annotation project.

Lexical borrowings can be adapted (the spelling of the word is modified to comply with the phonological and orthographic patterns of the recipient language) or unadapted (the word preserves its original spelling). For this annotation task, adapted borrowings were ignored and only unadapted borrowings were annotated. Therefore, Spanish adaptations of anglicisms like *fútbol* (from *football*), *mitin* (from *meeting*) and such were not annotated as borrowings. Similarly, words derived from foreign lexemes that do not comply with Spanish orthotactics but that have been morphologically derived following the Spanish paradigm (*hacktivista, hackear, shakespeariano*) were not annotated either. However, pseudo-anglicisms (words that are formed as if they were English, but do not exist in English, such as *footing* or *balconing*) were annotated.

Words that were not adapted but whose original spelling complies with graphophonological rules of Spanish (and are therefore unlikely to be ever adapted, such as *web, internet, fan, club, videoclip*) were annotated or not depending on how recent or emergent they were. After all, a word like *club*, that has been around in Spanish language for centuries, cannot be considered emergent anymore and, for this project, would not be as interesting to retrieve as real emerging anglicisms. The notion of *emergent* is, however, time-dependent and quite subjective: in order to determine which unadapted, graphophonologically acceptable borrowings were to be annotated, the online version of the *Diccionario de la lengua española*[4] (Real Academia

Española, 2014) was consulted. This dictionary is compiled by the Royal Spanish Academy, a prescriptive institution on Spanish language. This decision was motivated by the fact that, if a borrowing was already registered by this dictionary (that has conservative approach to language change) and is considered assimilated (that is, the institution recommended no italics or quotation marks to write that word) then it could be inferred that the word was not emergent anymore.

Although the previous guidelines covered most cases, they proved insufficient. Some anglicisms were unadapted (they preserved their original spelling), unacceptable according to the Spanish graphophonological rules, and yet did not satisfy the condition of being emergent. That was the case of words like *jazz* or *whisky*, words that do not comply with Spanish graphophonological rules but that were imported decades ago, cannot be considered emergent anymore and are unlikely to ever be adapted into the Spanish spelling system. To adjudicate these examples on those cases, the criterion of pragmatic markedness proposed by Winter-Froemel and Onysko (2012) (that distinguishes between catachrestic and non-catachrestic borrowing) was applied: if a borrowing was not adapted (i.e. its form remained exactly as it came from English) but referred to a particular invention or innovation that came via the English language, that was not perceived as new anymore and that had never competed with a Spanish equivalent, then it was ignored. This criteria proved to be extremely useful to deal with old unadapted anglicisms in the fields of music and food. Figure 1 summarizes the decision steps followed during the annotation process.

The corpus was annotated by a native speaker of Spanish using Doccano[5] (Nakayama et al., 2018). The annotation tagset includes two labels: ENG, to annotate the English borrowings just described, and OTHER. This OTHER tag was used to tag lexical borrowings from languages other than English. After all, although English is today by far the most prevalent donor of borrowings, there are other languages that also provide new borrowings to Spanish. Furthermore, the tag OTHER allows to annotate borrowings such as *première* or *tempeh*, borrowings that etymologically do not come from English but that have entered the Spanish language via English influence, even when their spelling is very different to English borrowings. In general, we considered that having such a tag could also help assess how successful a classifier is detecting foreign borrowings in general in Spanish newswire (without having to create a label for every possible donor language, as the number of examples would be too sparse). In total, the training set contained 40 entities labeled as OTHER, the development set contained 14 and the test set contained 13. The supplemental test set contained 35 OTHER entities.

5. Baseline Model

A baseline model for automatic extraction of anglicisms was created using the annotated corpus we just presented as training material. As mentioned in Section 3, the task of detecting anglicisms can be approached as a sequence

---

[4] https://dle.rae.es/

[5] https://github.com/chakki-works/doccano

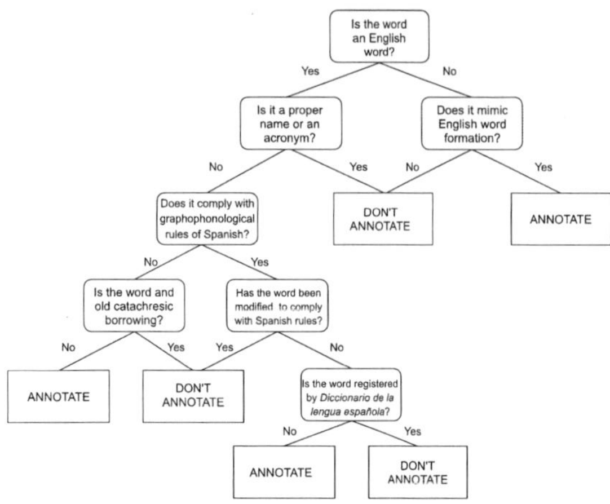

Figure 1: Decision steps to follow during the annotation process to decide whether to annotate a word as a borrowing.

labeling problem where only certain spans of texts will be labeled as anglicism (in a similar way to an NER task). The chosen model was conditional random field model (CRF), which was also the most popular model in both Shared Tasks on Language Identification for Code-Switched Data (Molina et al., 2016; Solorio et al., 2014).

The model was built using `pycrfsuite`[6] (Korobov and Peng, 2014), the Python wrapper for `crfsuite`[7] (Okazaki, 2007) that implements CRF for labeling sequential data. It also used the `Token` and `Span` utilities from `spaCy`[8] library (Honnibal and Montani, 2017).

The following handcrafted features were used for the model:

- Bias feature

- Token feature

- Uppercase feature (y/n)

- Titlecase feature (y/n)

- Character trigram feature

- Quotation feature (y/n)

- Word suffix feature (last three characters)

- POS tag (provided by `spaCy` utilities)

- Word shape (provided by `spaCy` utilities)

- Word embedding (see Table 3)

Given that anglicisms can be multiword expressions (such as *best seller, big data*) and that those units should be treated as one borrowing and not as two independent borrowings, we used multi-token BIO encoding to denote the

---

[6]https://github.com/scrapinghub/python-crfsuite
[7]https://github.com/chokkan/crfsuite
[8]https://spacy.io/

boundaries of each span (Ramshaw and Marcus, 1999). A window of two tokens in each direction was set for the feature extractor. The algorithm used was gradient descent with the L-BFGS method.

The model was tuned on the development set doing grid search; the hyperparameters considered were c1 (L1 regularization coefficient: 0.01, 0.05, 0.1, 0.5, 1.0), c2 (L2 regularization coefficient: 0.01, 0.05, 0.1, 0.5, 1.0), embedding scaling (0.5, 1.0, 2.0, 4.0), and embedding type (Bojanowski et al., 2017; Cañete, 2019; Cardellino, 2019; Grave et al., 2018; Honnibal and Montani, 2017; Pérez, 2017a; Pérez, 2017b) (see Table 3). The best results were obtained with c1 = 0.05, c2 = 0.01, scaling = 0.5 and word2vec Spanish embeddings by Cardellino (2019). The threshold for the stopping criterion delta was selected through observing the loss during preliminary experiments (delta = $1e-3$).

Author	Algorithm	# Vectors	Dimensions
Bojanowski et al. (2017)	FastText	985,667	300
Cañete (2019)	FastText	1,313,423	300
Cardellino (2019)	word2vec	1,000,653	300
Grave et al. (2018)	FastText	2,000,001	300
Honnibal and Montani (2017)	word2vec	534,000	50
Pérez (2017a)	FastText	855,380	300
Pérez (2017b)	GloVe	855,380	300

Table 3: Types of embeddings tried.

In order to assess the significance of the the handcrafted features, a feature ablation study was done on the tuned model, ablating one feature at a time and testing on the development set. Due to the scarcity of spans labeled with the OTHER tag on the development set (only 14) and given that the main purpose of the model is to detect anglicisms, the baseline model was run ignoring the OTHER tag both during tuning and the feature ablation experiments. Table 4 displays the results on the development set with all features and for the different feature ablation runs. The results show that all features proposed for the baseline model contribute to the results, with the character trigram feature being the one that has the biggest impact on the feature ablation study.

Features	Precision	Recall	F1 score	F1 change
All features	97.84	**82.65**	**89.60**	
− Bias	96.76	81.74	88.61	−0.99
− Token	95.16	80.82	87.41	−2.19
− Uppercase	97.30	82.19	89.11	−0.49
− Titlecase	96.79	**82.65**	89.16	−0.44
− Char trigram	96.05	77.63	85.86	−3.74
− Quotation	97.31	**82.65**	89.38	−0.22
− Suffix	97.30	82.19	89.11	−0.49
− POS tag	**98.35**	81.74	89.28	−0.32
− Word shape	96.79	**82.65**	89.16	−0.44
− Word embedding	95.68	80.82	87.62	−1.98

Table 4: Ablation study results on the development test.

6. Results

The baseline model was then run on the test set and the supplemental test set with the set of features and hyperparameters mentioned on Section 5. Table 5 displays the results obtained. The model was run both with and without the OTHER tag. The metrics for ENG display the results obtained only for the spans labeled as anglicisms; the metrics for OTHER display the results obtained for any borrowing other than anglicisms. The metrics for BORROWING discard the type of label and consider correct any labeled span that has correct boundaries, regardless of the label type (so any type of borrowing, regardless if it is ENG or OTHER). In all cases, only full matches were considered correct and no credit was given to partial matching, i.e. if only *fake* in *fake news* was retrieved, it was considered wrong and no partial score was given.

Results on all sets show an important difference between precision and recall, precision being significantly higher than recall. There is also a significant difference between the results obtained on development and test set (F1 = 89.60, F1 = 87.82) and the results on the supplemental test set (F1 = 71.49). The time difference between the supplemental test set and the development and test set (the headlines from the the supplemental test set being from a different time period to the training set) can probably explain these differences.

Comparing the results with and without the OTHER tag, it seems that including it on the development and test set produces worse results (or they remain roughly the same, at best). However, the best precision result on the supplemental test was obtained when including the OTHER tag and considering both ENG and OTHER spans as BORROWING (precision = 87.62). This is caused by the fact that, while the development and test set were compiled from anglicism-rich newspaper sections (similar to the training set), the supplemental test set contained headlines from all the sections in the newspaper, and therefore included borrowings from other languages such as Catalan, Basque or French. When running the model without the OTHER tag on the supplemental test set, these non-English borrowings were labeled as anglicisms by the model (after all, their spelling does not resemble Spanish spelling), damaging the precision score. When the OTHER tag was included, these non-English borrowings got correctly labeled as OTHER, improving the precision score. This proves that, although the OTHER tag might be irrelevant or even damaging when testing on the development or test set, it can be useful when testing on more naturalistic data, such as the one in the supplemental test set.

Concerning errors, two types of errors were recurrent among all sets: long titles of songs, films or series written in English were a source of false positives, as the model tended to mistake some of the uncapitalized words in the title for anglicisms (for example, *it darker* in "'You want it darker', la oscura y brillante despedida de Leonard Cohen"). On the other hand, anglicisms that appear on the first position of the sentence (and were, therefore, capitalized) were consistently ignored (as the model probably assumed they were named entities) and produced a high number of false negatives (for example, *vamping* in "Vamping: la recurrente leyenda urbana de la luz azul 'asesina'").

The results on Table 5 cannot, however, be compared to the ones reported by previous work: the metric that we report

Set	Precision	Recall	F1 score
Development set (− OTHER)	97.84	82.65	89.60
Development set (+ OTHER)			
ENG	96.79	82.65	89.16
OTHER	100.0	28.57	44.44
BORROWING	96.86	79.40	87.26
Test set (− OTHER)	95.05	81.60	87.82
Test set (+ OTHER)			
ENG	95.03	81.13	87.53
OTHER	100.0	46.15	63.16
BORROWING	95.19	79.11	86.41
Supplemental test set (− OTHER)	83.16	62.70	71.49
Supplemental test set (+ OTHER)			
ENG	82.65	64.29	72.32
OTHER	100.0	20.0	33.33
BORROWING	87.62	57.14	69.17

Table 5: Results on test set and supplemental test set.

is span F-measure, as the evaluation was done on span level (instead of token level) and credit was only given to full matches. Secondly, there was no Spanish tag assigned to non-borrowings, that means that no credit was given if a Spanish token was identified as such.

7. Future Work

This is an on-going project. The corpus we have just presented is a first step towards the development of an extractor of emerging anglicisms in the Spanish press. Future work includes: assessing whether to keep the OTHER tag, improving the baseline model (particularly to improve recall), assessing the suitability and contribution of different sets of features and exploring different models. In terms of the corpus development, the training set is now closed and stable, but the test set could potentially be increased in order to have more and more diverse anglicisms.

8. Conclusions

In this paper we have presented a new corpus of 21,570 newspaper headlines written in European Spanish. The corpus is annotated with emergent anglicisms and, up to our very best knowledge, is the first corpus of this type to be released publicly. We have presented the annotation scope, tagset and guidelines, and we have introduced a CRF baseline model for anglicism extraction trained with the described corpus. The results obtained show that the the corpus and baseline model are appropriate for automatic anglicism extraction.

9. Acknowledgements

The author would like to thank Constantine Lignos for his feedback and advice on this project.

10. Bibliographical References

Aguilar, G., AlGhamdi, F., Soto, V., Diab, M., Hirschberg, J., and Solorio, T. (2018). Named entity recognition on code-switched data: Overview of the CALCS 2018 shared task. In *Proceedings of the Third Workshop on Computational Approaches to Linguistic Code-Switching*, pages 138–147, Melbourne, Australia, July. Association for Computational Linguistics.

Al-Badrashiny, M. and Diab, M. (2016). The George Washington University System for the Code-Switching Workshop Shared Task 2016. In *Proceedings of the Second Workshop on Computational Approaches to Code Switching*, pages 108–111, Austin, Texas, November. Association for Computational Linguistics.

Alex, B., Dubey, A., and Keller, F. (2007). Using foreign inclusion detection to improve parsing performance. In *Proceedings of the 2007 Joint Conference on Empirical Methods in Natural Language Processing and Computational Natural Language Learning (EMNLP-CoNLL)*, pages 151–160.

Alex, B. (2008a). *Automatic detection of English inclusions in mixed-lingual data with an application to parsing*. Ph.D. thesis, University of Edinburgh.

Alex, B. (2008b). Comparing corpus-based to web-based lookup techniques for automatic English inclusion detection. In *Proceedings of the Sixth International Conference on Language Resources and Evaluation (LREC'08)*, Marrakech, Morocco, May. European Language Resources Association (ELRA).

Andersen, G. (2012). Semi-automatic approaches to Anglicism detection in Norwegian corpus data. In Cristiano Furiassi, et al., editors, *The anglicization of European lexis*, pages 111–130.

Balteiro, I. (2011). A reassessment of traditional lexicographical tools in the light of new corpora: sports anglicisms in Spanish. *International Journal of English Studies*, 11(2):23–52.

Bojanowski, P., Grave, E., Joulin, A., and Mikolov, T. (2017). Enriching word vectors with subword information. *Transactions of the Association for Computational Linguistics*, 5:135–146.

Chesley, P. and Baayen, R. H. (2010). Predicting new words from newer words: Lexical borrowings in French. *Linguistics*, 48(6):1343.

Clyne, M., Clyne, M. G., and Michael, C. (2003). *Dynamics of language contact: English and immigrant languages*. Cambridge University Press.

De la Cruz Cabanillas, I. and Martínez, C. T. (2012). Email or correo electrónico? Anglicisms in Spanish. *Revista española de lingüística aplicada*, (1):95–118.

Diéguez, M. I. (2004). El anglicismo léxico en el discurso económico de divulgación científica del español de Chile. *Onomázein*, 2(10):117–141.

Furiassi, C. and Hofland, K. (2007). The retrieval of false anglicisms in newspaper texts. In *Corpus Linguistics 25 Years On*, pages 347–363. Brill Rodopi.

Garley, M. and Hockenmaier, J. (2012). Beefmoves: Dissemination, diversity, and dynamics of English borrowings in a German hip hop forum. In *Proceedings of the 50th Annual Meeting of the Association for Computational Linguistics (Volume 2: Short Papers)*, pages 135–139, Jeju Island, Korea, July. Association for Computational Linguistics.

Gerding, C., Fuentes, M., Gómez, L., and Kotz, G. (2014). Anglicism: An active word-formation mechanism in Spanish. *Colombian Applied Linguistics Journal*, 16(1):40–54.

Gerding Salas, C., Cañete González, P., and Adam, C. (2018). Neología sintagmática anglicada en español: Calcos y préstamos. *Revista signos*, 51(97):175–192.

Gómez Capuz, J. (1997). Towards a typological classification of linguistic borrowing (illustrated with anglicisms in romance languages). *Revista alicantina de estudios ingleses*, 10:81–94.

Grave, E., Bojanowski, P., Gupta, P., Joulin, A., and Mikolov, T. (2018). Learning word vectors for 157 languages. In *Proceedings of the International Conference on Language Resources and Evaluation (LREC 2018)*.

Gómez Capuz, J. (2004). *Los préstamos del español: lengua y sociedad*. Cuadernos de Lengua Española. Arco Libros.

Haspelmath, M. (2008). Loanword typology: Steps toward a systematic cross-linguistic study of lexical borrowability. *Empirical Approaches to Language Typology*, 35:43.

Hofland, K. (2000). A self-expanding corpus based on newspapers on the web. In *Proceedings of the Second International Conference on Language Resources and Evaluation (LREC'00)*, Athens, Greece, May. European Language Resources Association (ELRA).

Jaech, A., Mulcaire, G., Ostendorf, M., and Smith, N. A. (2016). A neural model for language identification in code-switched tweets. In *Proceedings of the Second Workshop on Computational Approaches to Code Switching*, pages 60–64, Austin, Texas, November. Association for Computational Linguistics.

Lipski, J. M. (2005). Code-switching or borrowing? No sé so no puedo decir, you know. In *Selected proceedings of the second workshop on Spanish sociolinguistics*, pages 1–15. Cascadilla Proceedings Project Somerville, MA.

Lorenzo, E. (1996). *Anglicismos hispánicos*. Biblioteca románica hispánica: Estudios y ensayos. Gredos.

Losnegaard, G. S. and Lyse, G. I. (2012). A data-driven approach to anglicism identification in Norwegian. In Gisle Andersen, editor, *Exploring Newspaper Language: Using the web to create and investigate a large corpus of modern Norwegian*, pages 131–154. John Benjamins Publishing.

Medina López, J. (1998). *El anglicismo en el español actual*. Cuadernos de lengua española. Arco Libros.

Menéndez, F., Menéndez, M., and Morales, H. (2003). *El desplazamiento lingüístico del español por el inglés*. Cátedra lingüística. Cátedra.

Molina, G., AlGhamdi, F., Ghoneim, M., Hawwari, A., Rey-Villamizar, N., Diab, M., and Solorio, T. (2016). Overview for the second shared task on language identification in code-switched data. In *Proceedings of the Second Workshop on Computational Approaches to Code Switching*, pages 40–49, Austin, Texas, November. Association for Computational Linguistics.

Moreno Fernández, F. and Moreno Sandoval, A. (2018). Configuración lingüística de anglicismos procedentes de Twitter en el español estadounidense. *Revista signos*, 51(98):382–409.

Núñez Nogueroles, E. E. (2016). Anglicisms in CREA: a quantitative analysis in Spanish newspapers. *Language design: journal of theoretical and experimental linguistics*, 18:0215–242.

Núñez Nogueroles, E. (2017a). An up-to-date review of the literature on anglicisms in spanish. *Diálogo de la Lengua, IX*, pages 1–54.

Núñez Nogueroles, E. E. (2017b). Typographical, orthographic and morphological variation of anglicisms in a corpus of Spanish newspaper texts. *Revista Canaria de Estudios Ingleses*, (75):175–190.

Núñez Nogueroles, E. E. (2018a). A comprehensive definition and typology of anglicisms in present-day Spanish. *Epos: Revista de filología*, (34):211–237.

Núñez Nogueroles, E. E. (2018b). A corpus-based study of anglicisms in the 21st century spanish press. *Analecta Malacitana (AnMal electrónica)*, (44):123–159.

Oncíns Martínez, J. L. (2012). Newly-coined anglicisms in contemporary Spanish. a corpus-based approach. In Cristiano Furiassi, et al., editors, *The anglicization of European lexis*, pages 217–238.

Onysko, A. (2007). *Anglicisms in German: Borrowing, lexical productivity, and written codeswitching*, volume 23. Walter de Gruyter.

Patzelt, C. (2011). The impact of English on Spanish-language media in the usa. In *Multilingual Discourse Production: Diachronic and Synchronic Perspectives*, volume 12, page 257. John Benjamins Publishing.

Poplack, S. and Dion, N. (2012). Myths and facts about loanword development. *Language Variation and Change*, 24(3):279–315.

Poplack, S., Sankoff, D., and Miller, C. (1988). The social correlates and linguistic processes of lexical borrowing and assimilation. *Linguistics*, 26(1):47–104.

Poplack, S. (2012). What does the nonce borrowing hypothesis hypothesize? *Bilingualism: Language and Cognition*, 15(3):644–648.

Pratt, C. (1980). *El anglicismo en el español peninsular contemporáneo*, volume 308. Gredos.

Ramshaw, L. A. and Marcus, M. P. (1999). Text chunking using transformation-based learning. In *Natural language processing using very large corpora*, pages 157–176. Springer.

Rodríguez Medina, M. J. (2002). Los anglicismos de frecuencia sintácticos en español: estudio empírico. *RAEL. Revista electrónica de lingüística aplicada*.

Rodríguez González, F. (1999). Anglicisms in contemporary Spanish. an overview. *Atlantis*, 21(1/2):103–139.

Samih, Y., Maharjan, S., Attia, M., Kallmeyer, L., and Solorio, T. (2016). Multilingual code-switching identification via LSTM recurrent neural networks. In *Proceedings of the Second Workshop on Computational Approaches to Code Switching*, pages 50–59, Austin, Texas, November. Association for Computational Linguistics.

Serigos, J. (2017a). Using distributional semantics in loanword research: A concept-based approach to quantifying semantic specificity of anglicisms in Spanish. *International Journal of Bilingualism*, 21(5):521–540.

Serigos, J. R. L. (2017b). *Applying corpus and computational methods to loanword research: new approaches to Anglicisms in Spanish*. Ph.D. thesis, The University of Texas at Austin.

Shirvani, R., Piergallini, M., Gautam, G. S., and Chouikha, M. (2016). The Howard University System submission for the Shared Task in Language Identification in Spanish-English Codeswitching. In *Proceedings of the Second Workshop on Computational Approaches to Code Switching*, pages 116–120, Austin, Texas, November. Association for Computational Linguistics.

Shrestha, P. (2016). Codeswitching detection via lexical features in conditional random fields. In *Proceedings of the Second Workshop on Computational Approaches to Code Switching*, pages 121–126, Austin, Texas, November. Association for Computational Linguistics.

Sikdar, U. K. and Gambäck, B. (2016). Language identification in code-switched text using conditional random fields and Babelnet. In *Proceedings of the Second Workshop on Computational Approaches to Code Switching*, pages 127–131, Austin, Texas, November. Association for Computational Linguistics.

Solorio, T., Blair, E., Maharjan, S., Bethard, S., Diab, M., Ghoneim, M., Hawwari, A., AlGhamdi, F., Hirschberg, J., Chang, A., and Fung, P. (2014). Overview for the first shared task on language identification in code-switched data. In *Proceedings of the First Workshop on Computational Approaches to Code Switching*, pages 62–72, Doha, Qatar, October. Association for Computational Linguistics.

Tsvetkov, Y. and Dyer, C. (2016). Cross-lingual bridges with models of lexical borrowing. *Journal of Artificial Intelligence Research*, 55:63–93.

Vélez Barreiro, M. (2003). *Anglicismos en la prensa económica española*. Ph.D. thesis, Universidade da Coruña.

Winter-Froemel, E. and Onysko, A. (2012). Proposing a pragmatic distinction for lexical anglicisms. In Cristiano Furiassi, et al., editors, *The anglicization of European lexis*, page 43.

Xia, M. X. (2016). Codeswitching language identification using subword information enriched word vectors. In *Proceedings of the Second Workshop on Computational Approaches to Code Switching*, pages 132–136, Austin, Texas, November. Association for Computational Linguistics.

11. Language Resource References

Cardellino, Cristian. (2019). *Spanish Billion Words Corpus and Embeddings.* `https://crscardellino.github.io/SBWCE/`.

Cañete, José. (2019). *Spanish Word Embeddings.* Zenodo, `https://doi.org/10.5281/zenodo.3255001`.

Honnibal, Matthew and Montani, Ines. (2017). *spaCy 2: Natural language understanding with bloom embeddings, convolutional neural networks and incremental parsing.* `https://spacy.io/`.

Korobov, M and Peng, T. (2014). *Python-crfsuite.* `https://github.com/scrapinghub/python-crfsuite`.

Hiroki Nakayama and Takahiro Kubo and Junya Kamura and Yasufumi Taniguchi and Xu Liang. (2018). *doccano: Text Annotation Tool for Human.* `https://github.com/doccano/doccano`.

Naoaki Okazaki. (2007). *CRFsuite: a fast implementation of Conditional Random Fields (CRFs).* `http://www.chokkan.org/software/crfsuite/`.

Pérez, Jorge. (2017a). *FastText embeddings from SBWC.* Available at `https://github.com/dccuchile/spanish-word-embeddings#fasttext-embeddings-from-sbwc`.

Pérez, Jorge. (2017b). *GloVe embeddings from SBWC.* Available at `https://github.com/dccuchile/spanish-word-embeddings#glove-embeddings-from-sbwc`.

Real Academia Española. (2014). *Diccionario de la lengua española, ed. 23.3.* `http://dle.rae.es`.

Proceedings of the LREC 2020 – 4th Workshop on Computational Approaches to Code Switching, pages 9–16
Language Resources and Evaluation Conference (LREC 2020), Marseille, 11–16 May 2020
European Language Resources Association (ELRA), licensed under CC-BY-NC

A New Dataset for Natural Language Inference from Code-mixed Conversations

Simran Khanuja[a], Sandipan Dandapat[b], Sunayana Sitaram[a], Monojit Choudhury[a]
[a]Microsoft Research India, [b]Microsoft Corporation
Bangalore, India, Hyderabad, India
{t-sikha, sadandap, sunayana.sitaram, monojitc}@microsoft.com

Abstract

Natural Language Inference (NLI) is the task of inferring the logical relationship, typically entailment or contradiction, between a premise and hypothesis. Code-mixing is the use of more than one language in the same conversation or utterance, and is prevalent in multilingual communities all over the world. In this paper, we present the first dataset for code-mixed NLI, in which both the premises and hypotheses are in code-mixed Hindi-English. We use data from Hindi movies (Bollywood) as premises, and crowd-source hypotheses from Hindi-English bilinguals. We conduct a pilot annotation study and describe the final annotation protocol based on observations from the pilot. Currently, the data collected consists of 400 premises in the form of code-mixed conversation snippets and 2240 code-mixed hypotheses. We conduct an extensive analysis to infer the linguistic phenomena commonly observed in the dataset obtained. We evaluate the dataset using a standard mBERT-based pipeline for NLI and report results.

Keywords: code-switching, natural language inference, dataset

1. Introduction

Natural Language Inference (NLI) is a fundamental NLP task, not only because it has several practical applications, but also because it tests the language understanding abilities of machines beyond pattern recognition. NLI tasks usually involve inferring the logical relationship, such as entailment or contradiction, between a pair of sentences. In some cases, instead of a sentence, a document, paragraph or a dialogue snippet might be provided as the *premise*; the task then is to infer whether a given *hypothesis* is entailed in (or implied by) the premise. There are several monolingual NLI datasets available, with the most notable ones being included in the GLUE (Wang et al., 2018) and SuperGLUE (Wang et al., 2019) benchmarks. There are also multilingual and crosslingual NLI datasets, such as XNLI (Conneau et al., 2018). These datasets have successfully spurred and facilitated research in this area.

In this paper, we introduce, for the first time, a new NLI dataset for *code-mixing*. Code-mixing or code-switching refers to the use of more than one language in a single conversation or utterance. It is prevalent in almost all multilingual societies across the world. Monolingual as well as multilingual NLP systems typically fail to handle code-mixed inputs. Therefore, recently, code-mixing has attained considerable attention from the speech and NLP communities. Consequently, there have been several shared tasks on language labeling, POS-tagging, and sentiment analysis of code-mixed text, and several datasets exist for these as well. Other speech and language processing tasks such as speech recognition, parsing, and question answering, have also been well researched upon. However, as far as we know, there exists no code-mixed dataset for any NLI task.

The following reasons explain the motivation behind creating a code-mixed NLI dataset:

- NLI is an important requirement for chatbots and conversational agents, and since code-mixing is a spoken and conversational phenomenon, it is crucial that such systems understand code-mixing.

- Most NLI datasets, including monolingual datasets, are created using sentence pairs as the premise and hypothesis. Ours is one of the only datasets built on conversations as premises, which, we believe, facilitates improved consistency in dialogue agents.

- NLI helps indicate whether our models can truly understand code-mixing, as the task requires a deeper semantic understanding of language rather than reliance upon shallow heuristics.

To create the code-mixed NLI dataset, we use pre-existing code-mixed conversations from Hindi movies (*Bollywood*) as premises, and ask crowd-workers to annotate the data with hypotheses that are either *entailed in* or *contradicted by* the premise. We follow this with a validation step where annotators are shown premises and hypotheses and are asked to validate whether the hypothesis is *entailed in* or *contradicted by* the corresponding premise. We conduct a pilot experiment and present its analysis with the final annotation scheme and a description of the data collection process. Currently our data consists of 400 premises with 2240 hypotheses in code-mixed *Hindi-English*.

The rest of the paper is organized as follows. Section 2 introduces different NLI datasets and situates our work in their context. Section 3 describes the creation of the data for annotation. Section 4 describes the data annotation, including results from the pilot and the final annotation scheme. Section 5 presents an extensive analysis and a baseline evaluation. Section 6 concludes with a discussion of future work.

2. NLI Datasets

NLI is a concept central to natural language understanding models. Most of the prominent datasets that are used to solve NLI problems involve learning textual entailment wherein we determine whether a hypothesis is entailed in or contradicts a textual document (Zhang and Chai, 2009).

Conversation	Translation
MRS.KAPOOR: Kitna old fashion hairstyle hai tumhara, new hair cut kyun nahin try karte .. Go to the Vidal Sasoon salon tomorrow .. Aur thoda product use karo .. You'll get some texture.	MRS KAPOOR: Your hairstyle is so old fashioned, why don't you try a new hair cut .. Go to the Vidal Sasoon salon tomorrow .. And use some product .. You'll get some texture.
MR.KAPOOR: Tumhari maa ko bahut pata hai, MBA kiya hai usne hair styling mein.	MR.KAPOOR: Your mother knows a lot, she has done an MBA in hair styling.
MRS.KAPOOR: Kaash kiya hota to tumhara kuch kar pati? Kab se ke rahi hun, Soonawallas ki tarah hair transplant karva lo, already 55 ke lagte ho!	MRS.KAPOOR: I wish I had so that I could have done something about you? Been telling you for so long, get a hair transplant like the Soonawallas, you already look like you are 55!
MR.KAPOOR: main 57 ka hun.	MR.KAPOOR: I am 57 years old.

Table 1: Example Conversation from the Bollywood data

Even so, each dataset is severely limited in the reasoning it represents and cannot be generalised outside of its domain. (Bernardy and Chatzikyriakidis, 2019)

2.1. Types of NLI Datasets

We briefly outline the prominent NLI datasets that have been well researched upon, to suitably place our contribution in context of the same.

- The FraCaS test suite (Consortium and others, 1996) consists of 346 manually curated premises followed by a *Yes/No/Don't Know* question.

- The RTE datasets (Dagan et al., 2005) include naturally occurring data as premises and construct hypotheses based on them. All datasets have fewer than 1000 examples for training. A limitation of these datasets is that many examples assume world knowledge which is not explicitly labeled with each example.

- The SNLI dataset (Bowman et al., 2015) consists of 570k inference pairs created using crowd-sourcing on Amazon Mechanical Turk. The size of this dataset makes it conducive to be used for training deep learning models. Subjects are given the caption of an image and are asked to formulate a *true* caption, a *possible true* caption and a *false* caption.

- The Multi-Genre NLI corpus (Williams et al., 2017) is also a crowd-sourced collection of 433k sentence pairs annotated with entailment information. Although it is modeled on SNLI, it differs from it as it covers a variety of genres in both written and spoken English. XNLI (Conneau et al., 2018) is a multilingual extension of MultiNLI wherein 5k (train) and 2.5k (dev) examples are translated into 14 languages.

- The SICK (Sentences Involving Compositional Knowledge) (Marelli et al., 2014) dataset consists of 9840 examples of inference patterns primarily to test distributional semantics. It is constructed by randomly selecting a subset of sentence pairs from two sources - the 8k ImageFlickr dataset and the SemEval2012 STS MSR-Video Description dataset.

- The Dialogue NLI Corpus (Welleck et al., 2018) consists of pairs of sentences generated using the Persona-Chat dataset (Zhang et al., 2018). Each human labeled triple is first associated to each persona sentence and then pairs of such triple; persona sentences are labeled as entailment, neutral or contradiction. The corpus consists of around 33k examples.

- The Conversation Entailment (Zhang and Chai, 2010) dataset consists of 50 dialogues from the Switchboard corpus (Godfrey et al., 1992). 15 volunteer annotators read the dialogues and manually created hypotheses to obtain a total of 1096 entailment annotated examples.

While most of the datasets described above benefit information extraction and other textual analysis problems, they cannot be used to tackle inference in conversations, which is an important application today given the upsurge and importance of dialogue agents. (Bernardy and Chatzikyriakidis, 2019) make a strong case for the need of entailment datasets for dialogue data, highlighting that there has been no attempt towards building one so far. They point out several ways in which conversation entailment is different from textual entailment. Most importantly, each participant in the conversation adds more structure to the segment in his/her turn unlike textual entailment where one segment is stand-alone.

Consider the example below from (Bernardy and Chatzikyriakidis, 2019):

A. Mont Blanc is higher than
B. Mt. Ararat?
A. Yes.
B. No, this is not correct. It is the other way around.
A. Are you...
B. Sure? Yes, I am.
A. Ok, then

Further, with the exception of the XNLI dataset, all other NLI datasets are in English. This motivates us to use dialogue, or conversation, as a premise, and build hypotheses based on them for code-mixed language. Based on the approaches used for creating the datasets mentioned above, there are three main approaches that can be taken while creating a code-mixed NLI dataset. One approach is to translate an existing NLI dataset into a code-mixed language. Since there do not exist good Machine Translation systems for code-mixed languages, that can capture the nuances of the language necessary for an NLI dataset, this would need to be done manually to ensure high quality. Another approach is to synthesize code-mixed data artificially, using approaches such as (Pratapa et al., 2018). However, this cannot be done for a conversational dataset, and will not be natural enough to create good hypotheses. The third approach, which we take, is to use a naturally occurring source of conversational data as premises, and get the hypotheses manually annotated.

3. Dataset Creation

Code-mixing is primarily a spoken language phenomenon, so it is challenging to find naturally occurring code-mixed text on the web, or in standard monolingual corpora. Social Media and Instant Messaging data from multilingual users can be a source of code-mixed conversational data, but cannot be used due to privacy concerns. For this reason, we choose scripts of Hindi movies, also referred to as "Bollywood" movies. Bollywood movies, from certain time periods and genres, contain varying amounts of code-mixing, as described in (Pratapa and Choudhury, 2017). Although the movie data is not artificially generated, it is scripted, which makes it a less natural source of data than conversations between real people.

3.1. Data Preparation

The Bollywood data consists of scenes taken from 18 movies. The data is in Romanized form, so both Hindi and English parts of the conversation are written in the Roman script. Table 1 shows an example conversation from the Bollywood dataset. The data contains examples of both inter-sentential and intra-sentential code-mixing.

Based upon an initial manual inspection of the data, we make the following design choices :

- There are 1803 scenes in the 18 movie transcripts combined. We observe that a few scenes are monologues, reducing the problem from a conversational entailment to a textual one. Hence we use an initial filter of choosing scenes with greater than three number of turns.

- A number of scenes were in monolingual Hindi, this being a Bollywood movie dataset. Hence we calculate the *Code Mixing Index (CMI)* (Gambäck and Das, 2014) of each scene and choose scenes having a CMI greater than 20%. After application of the above filters, we obtain 720 scenes.

- We choose not to transliterate the Romanized Hindi into the original Devanagari script. However, this can

be done automatically using a transliteration system if desired.

3.2. Task Paradigm

The data annotation process involves the formulation of one or more true and false hypothesis, given a scene from the categories above as a premise. Subsequently, the NLI task is to classify whether the conversation entails the hypothesis or contradicts it, which we label true and false respectively. Note that the premises and the formulated hypotheses are in code-mixed *Hindi-English*.

4. Data Annotation

4.1. Initial Annotation Guidelines

Our annotation scheme consists of two stages. In the first stage, we present conversations with a set of already created hypotheses (cf. Table 3) and ask the annotators to assign two labels to each hypothesis statement. The first is a *true/false* label and the second is a *good/fair/bad* label, judging the quality of the given hypothesis. Table 2 shows details of the two different labels used in the annotation process.

Annotators were also instructed to assign an *Irrelevant* label in case the generated hypothesis is not relevant to the conversation. In general, a hypothesis is considered as irrelevant when there is not enough topic and word overlap between the statement of the hypothesis and the conversation, especially when generating negative hypotheses, or when world knowledge is used to formulate the hypothesis, which cannot be inferred from the conversation.

The first stage is conducted to fulfil two objectives:

- It acts as an initial filter to make sure that the annotators are well versed in both languages and have a good understanding of the task. If they fail to assign gold labels to more than 80 percent of the hypotheses, they will not be assigned the second stage of annotation.

- It serves to show annotators, the kind of hypotheses we are expecting will be generated from the conversations.

In the second stage, the annotators are given only the conversation snippet and are asked to come up with hypotheses which they think are *entailed in* or *contradicted by* the conversation. We provide annotators with a guideline containing worked out examples to make them familiar with the classification and help them generate good hypotheses. These hypotheses could be written in Hindi, English or both languages mixed in one sentence, as people often do in informal settings. Note that since the conversation contains Romanized Hindi, we ask the annotators to write Hindi in the Roman script. Romanized Hindi is not standardized, so we find variations of the same word across the Bollywood data. The annotators were asked to use spelling variants that they found in the snippets, or use the variants they are most familiar with.

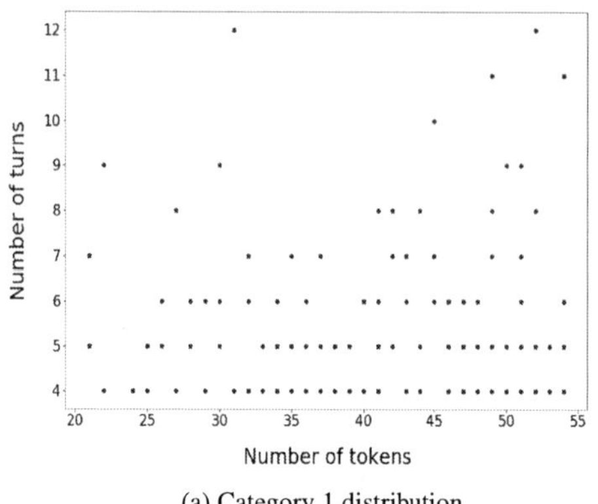

(a) Category 1 distribution

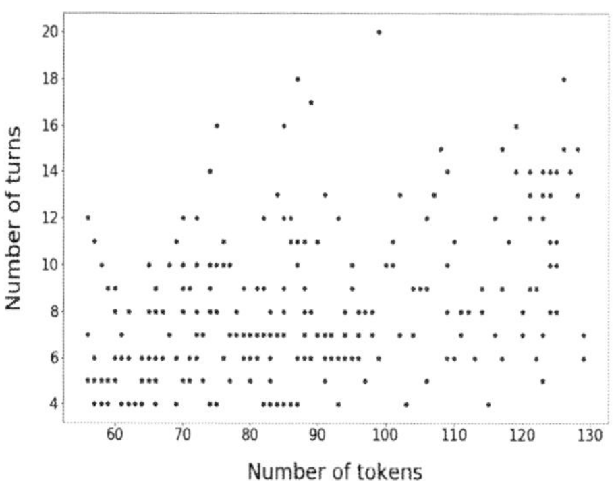

(b) Category 2 distribution

Figure 1: Distribution of data in different categories

Label	Categories	Definition
Label1	True	It can be inferred from the conversation (entailed)
	False	It is contradictory to the conversation
	Good	An unambiguous statement which can clearly
		be either inferred from the conversation or stands contradictory to it
Label2	Fair	Can be fairly inferred/contradicted from the conversation
		but lacks in either a good structure/is too long/is too abstract
		contains too many(or too few) words from the snippet
	Bad	A statement which isn't well-formed/ is too ambiguous
		or is verbatim from the conversation

Table 2: Types of labels

4.2. Pilot Experiments

In the pilot experiment, for the first stage, we use 2 conversations of different lengths (7 and 17 turns) having a set of carefully curated hypotheses (8 and 10 respectively). The task is to mark each hypothesis with Label1 (True/False/Irrelevant) and Label2 (Good/Fair/Bad). On an average, the number of correct labels is 88%.

For the second stage, we take 3 conversation snippets of different lengths (9, 12 and 13 turns) and ask the annotators to generate 4 hypotheses (2 True and 2 False) for each conversation. 7 different annotators conduct the task.

Our observations from the pilot are as follows:

- Annotators do not prefer long premises as they need to go back and forth to validate the correctness of a statement. However, too short a premise also does not provide enough context for the annotators to come up with good hypotheses.

- Annotators face difficulty in producing a large number of hypotheses. The average amount of time required to produce a hypothesis increases non-linearly with the number of hypotheses expected from a conversation.

- A few annotators use prior knowledge about the topic (i.e. the movie is known to the annotator). This leads to the generation of bad hypotheses or incorrect labeling.

4.3. Final Scheme and Guidelines

Based on the observations from the pilot experiments, we make the following changes into the annotation process:

- **Length of the Premises**: We segregate the conversations into three categories based on the number of tokens they contain, to obtain 151 scenes that contain less than 55 tokens (Category 1), 252 scenes that contain less than 130 tokens (Category 2), and the rest containing more than 130 tokens (Category 3). We consider conversations from Categories 1 and 2 for annotation, based on the observation that annotators find it increasingly time-consuming to formulate hypotheses for very long conversations. Figures 1 (a) and (b) give a pictorial representation of conversations in Category 1 and 2, with *number of tokens* on the X axis and *number of turns* on the Y axis.

- **Number of Hypotheses**: Depending on the length of the premises, the annotators are asked to generate different number of hypotheses. The required number of hypotheses is 2 (one True and one False) if a conversation is from Category 1 (between 20-55 tokens) and 4 (two each for True and False) if taken from Category 2 (between 55 and 130 tokens). However, the annotators have the option to generate additional hypotheses if they desire.

Category	Hypothesis	Translation
True	Mr. Kapoor 57 years ke hai	Mr. Kapoor is 57 years old
False	Mrs. Kapoor ne hair styling mei MBA kiya hai	Mrs. Kapoor has done an MBA in hair styling
Bad	Mr. Kapoor will go to the Vidal Sasoon salon tomorrow	
Irrelevant	Mr. Kapoor was born in Delhi.	
Ambiguous	Mrs. Kapoor ko hair styling ke baare mei bohot pata hai	Mrs. Kapoor knows a lot about hair styling

Table 3: Different kinds of hypotheses for the conversation snippet in Table 1

- **De-biasing**: Bias in NLI datasets is well studied (Rudinger et al., 2017) and can be attributed to annotators amplifying stereotypical characteristics of the conversation participants. In our case, there is additional bias due to the knowledge of the movie, which can be inferred from the names of some characters, and sometimes from the conversation. To handle the latter, we anonymize the names of the turn owners and replace them with generic tokens ("C1", "C2" etc.). In this process, we only substitute the proper names from the conversation and not the kinship terms (*Father, Mother, Bauji etc.*) or professions (*Doctor, Receptionist, Police Officer etc.*). This helps reduce the familiarity of the conversation with a known movie which produces noise in the pilot study (cf. Section 4.2).

4.4. Final Annotation Process

The final hypotheses generation process is as follows:

- First, an annotator is shown the conversation after making the changes described above, and asked to formulate 2 or 4 hypotheses depending on the length of the conversation. Currently, we have 600 hypotheses created from 150 premises in Category 1 (length between 20-55 tokens) and another 1640 hypotheses created from 250 premises in Category 2 (length between 55-130 tokens).

- Subsequently, we conduct a validation step in which two annotators are shown 300 conversation snippets and corresponding hypotheses, and asked to mark the hypotheses "True" (entailed),"False" (contradicted) or "Irrelevant". The Inter-Annotator Agreement is 0.863, and the agreement of each annotator with the labels of the generated hypotheses is greater than 0.8, which shows that the data collected is of good quality.

5. Analysis and Evaluation

On a deeper analysis of the hypotheses generated, we make the following observations:

- **Sarcasm and Rhetorics**: Several examples require the model to interpret sarcasm in the conversation, to make a correct prediction. This is natural, given the premises are human conversations, and these help add complexity to the dataset. For example -

PREMISE:
Mother: 5 saal baad saath-saath aaye ho .. janvaron ki tarah ladna zaroori hai ?

C0: Haan aapko toh main hi galat lagta hoon ..

HYPOTHESIS:
Mother told C0 to quarrel like animals. (*False*)

Translated

PREMISE:
Mother: Y'all have met after 5 years .. is it necessary to fight like animals?
C0: Yeah you always think I am wrong ..

HYPOTHESIS:
Mother told C0 to quarrel like animals. (*False*)

- **Word Sense Disambiguation** : There exist several examples requiring the model to resolve the meaning of the word in context of its usage. For example, in the following, the word "saala" is used as an abusive term in the premise, but is taken to mean "brother in law" in the hypothesis -

PREMISE:
C0: Ek lafz aur toh tera bheja baahar .
C1: Accha ? Nikaal .. Himmat hai to nikal C1 ka bheja baahar !
C1: Maar !
C0: Dekh be C1 . Aakhiri baar keh raha hoon ..
C1: Naqli Nawab saala ..

HYPOTHESIS:
C0 is C1's brother in law. (*False*)

Translated

PREMISE:
C0: One more word and I will smack your head.
C1: Really ? Hit .. If you have the strength, hit me !
C1: Hit !
C0: See C1 . I am telling you one last time ..
C1: Fool ..

HYPOTHESIS:
C0 is C1's brother in law. (*False*)

- **Inter-dependent Inference** : Several premises are such that each utterance is highly contextual, requiring knowledge of the speakers of the past few utterances as well. Hypotheses thus generated pick facts from several utterances at once. For example -

PREMISE:
C0: Kaun se school mein tha ?
C1: Bishop Cotton .
C0: Kahan hai ?
C1: Shimla ...

HYPOTHESIS:
Bishop Cotton School Manali mein hai. (*False*)

Translated

PREMISE:
C0: Which school were you in ?
C1: Bishop Cotton .
C0: Where is it ?
C1: Shimla ...

HYPOTHESIS:
Bishop Cotton School is in Manali. (*False*)

- **Domain Generality** : We also observe that this being a movie dataset, we obtain premise-hypothesis pairs across several domains. There even exist pairs with dialect differences as shown below :-

PREMISE:
C0: Chhorey tanne manaa karya tha na jaane se ?
C1: Koi milne aaya hai .
C0: Kaun ?
C0: Kaun sa ?
C1: Boli thaare se kaam tha

HYPOTHESIS:
C0 ne C1 ko jaane se mana kiya tha. (*True*)

Translated

PREMISE:
C0: Son, I had told you not to go right ?
C1: Somebody had come to meet me .
C0: Who ?
C0: Who was it ?
C1: She said she had some work for you

HYPOTHESIS:
C0 had told C1 not to go. (*True*)

- **Speaker Conflict**: We also observe examples wherein multiple parties hold different beliefs on a particular fact, hence inferring about the fact from the conversation becomes a difficult task. For example -

PREMISE:
C0: Waise main bhi uski tarah chest hila sakta hun.
C1: Show . See .. Nobody can beat him.

HYPOTHESIS:
C0 bhi uski tarah chest hila sakta hai. (*False*)

Translated

PREMISE:
C0: Even I can move my chest like him.
C1: Show . See .. Nobody can beat him.

HYPOTHESIS:
C0 can also move his chest like him. (*False*)

- **Paraphrasing**: In a few examples, true hypotheses are paraphrases of what was said in the conversation. In some cases, they are a substring of the conversation, but in other cases, they are paraphrased using code-mixing, or a single language when the premise uses the other language. This is usually observed in longer conversations. An example wherein the hypothesis is picked verbatim from the conversation is shown below :

PREMISE:
C0: Nahi Sir busy hain - voh nahi le saktey brief aapka !
C1: Lekin subah toh unhone kaha tha ki ...

HYPOTHESIS:
Sir busy hain. (*True*)

Translated

PREMISE:
C0: No, Sir is busy - He cannot take your brief !
C1: But in the morning he said that ...

HYPOTHESIS:
Sir is busy. (*True*)

- **Negation**: True or False hypotheses were negations of what was said in the conversation. For example -

PREMISE:
C0: Kahin bhi shuru ho jaati ho dance karna , shushma didi ki sagai hai ... relations mein hain humarey ... socha to karo ...
C1: Baaki ladkiyan bhi to kar rahi thi ...

HYPOTHESIS:
Baaki ladkiyan dance nahi kar rahi hai. (*False*)

Translated

PREMISE:
C0: You start dancing anywhere, It's sushma's reception ... they are our relatives... think sometimes
C1: But the other girls were dancing as well ...

HYPOTHESIS:
The other girls are not dancing. (*False*)

- **Swapping Roles**: We also observe cases wherein a false hypothesis is constructed by simply swapping for the speaker. For example -

Model	RTE	SNLI	MNLI	QNLI
$BERT_{BASE}$	66.4	90.4	86.7	90.5

Table 4: NLI results (Accuracy)

Model	NLI En-Hi
$mBERT$	57.82

Table 5: NLI results (Accuracy)

PREMISE:
C1: Jaan bhai ! Ab kya hoga ?
C0: Sab theek ho jaayega . Chup kar bus chup . Sab theek ho jaayega . Bank manager ko bol 10 karod cash chahiye kal subah

HYPOTHESIS:
C1 bol raha hai sab theek ho jaaega. (*False*)

Translated

PREMISE:
C1: Brother ! What will happen now ?
C0: Everything will be alright. Just be quiet. Everything will be alright. Tell the bank manager to arrange for 10 crore rupees by tomorrow morning.

HYPOTHESIS:
C1 says that everything will be alright. (*False*)

- **Numerical Hypotheses**: A few examples simply change a numeral in the premise to create a false hypothesis. For example -

PREMISE:
C2: Kitne saal se kaam kar rahe ho clinic mein ?
C1: 4 to ho gaye honge saab ..

HYPOTHESIS:
C2 5 saal se clinic mein kaam karta hai. (*False*)

Translated

PREMISE:
C2: For how many years have you been working at the clinic ?
C1: It must have been 4 years at the least, Sir ..

HYPOTHESIS:
C2 has been working at the clinic for 5 years. (*False*)

- **Length of Premise** : We also observe that for longer premises, annotators usually pick out sentences verbatim from the conversation. In general, the quality of the hypotheses generated decreases as the premises become longer.

- No hypotheses are found that are irrelevant or use world knowledge, or knowledge about the movies.

On the basis of the above observations, we see that the dataset obtained is highly varying in complexity. Models that rely on shallow heuristics and learn statistical patterns from training data, which is the case with most neural models today (McCoy et al., 2019), are expected to correctly predict examples involving *Negation*, *Numeral Changes*, *Swapping Roles* or *Paraphrasing*. However, they are hypothesized to fail in examples requiring deeper semantic knowledge, for instance, the examples involving *Sarcasm*, *Word Sense Disambiguation*, *Inter-dependent Inference* or *Speaker Conflict*.

With the recent upsurge of multilingual models, and claims that they can be used to solve code-mixed tasks as well, we evaluate the multilingual BERT model on our dataset. Previously, it has been shown to perform well on code-mixed POS tagging by (Pires et al., 2019). Our results are as shown in Table 5. We make use of the *transformers* library[1] for the experiment. We use the AdamW optimizer with a learning rate of 5e-5, epsilon of 1e-8, and a batch size of 16, as suggested by (Devlin et al., 2018). We train for 5 epochs. We report the average result of training on 5 random seed values. Note that the dataset contains Hindi in Roman script while mBERT is trained on Hindi in Devanagari, and we report this number as a mere baseline.

To put our numbers in perspective, we have included accuracies achieved by the BERT base model, as shown in (Talman and Chatzikyriakidis, 2018) and (Devlin et al., 2018), in Table 4 on standard monolingual NLI datasets. Note that these numbers are not directly comparable due to differences in language and corpus sizes. However, even standalone, the accuracy obtained by mBERT on our dataset clearly highlights the fact that this task is far from being solved.

6. Conclusion and Future Work

In this paper, we introduce a new dataset for code-mixed Natural Language Inference (NLI). Our dataset is unique due to the nature of the language used (code-mixed Hindi-English) and also because it is one of the few datasets created using conversations as premises. Solving the NLI task would help understand how well machines understand code-mixing. We also observe that multilingual models such as mBERT (Pires et al., 2019) are not competent enough to solve this task, thus highlighting the need for models especially suited for the task at hand. In future work, we plan to experiment with neural and symbolic architectures for code-mixed NLI. One challenge in testing

---

[1]https://github.com/huggingface/transformers

our data on models pre-trained on monolingual data is a script mismatch, as monolingual models tend to be trained on Devanagari, while our data contains Romanized Hindi with spelling variations.

Given the nature of the data, we observe that this dataset can be scaled up to generate a plethora of such premise hypothesis pairs. Noting the dearth of conversation entailment datasets in monolingual settings as well, the same can be done to create monolingual datasets. This can be a major contribution to help solve conversation inference tasks which can show significant improvements in existing conversational agents.

Currently, our dataset consists of 400 premises with 2240 hypotheses, labeled for True and False only. We plan to continue the annotation process with more such transcripts. Further, we plan to further annotate the dataset for other linguistic phenomena, which may help to better solve the task. We plan to release the annotations we have crowd-sourced for research purposes and hope that it will spur research in the field of code-mixed NLI.

7. Bibliographical References

Bernardy, J.-P. and Chatzikyriakidis, S. (2019). What kind of natural language inference are nlp systems learning: Is this enough?

Bowman, S. R., Angeli, G., Potts, C., and Manning, C. D. (2015). A large annotated corpus for learning natural language inference. *arXiv preprint arXiv:1508.05326*.

Conneau, A., Lample, G., Rinott, R., Williams, A., Bowman, S. R., Schwenk, H., and Stoyanov, V. (2018). Xnli: Evaluating cross-lingual sentence representations. *arXiv preprint arXiv:1809.05053*.

Consortium, F. et al. (1996). Using the framework. *Fracas project LRE 62*, 51.

Dagan, I., Glickman, O., and Magnini, B. (2005). The pascal recognising textual entailment challenge. In *Machine Learning Challenges Workshop*, pages 177–190. Springer.

Devlin, J., Chang, M.-W., Lee, K., and Toutanova, K. (2018). Bert: Pre-training of deep bidirectional transformers for language understanding. *arXiv preprint arXiv:1810.04805*.

Gambäck, B. and Das, A. (2014). On measuring the complexity of code-mixing. ICON.

Godfrey, J. J., Holliman, E. C., and McDaniel, J. (1992). Switchboard: Telephone speech corpus for research and development. In *[Proceedings] ICASSP-92: 1992 IEEE International Conference on Acoustics, Speech, and Signal Processing*, volume 1, pages 517–520. IEEE.

Marelli, M., Bentivogli, L., Baroni, M., Bernardi, R., Menini, S., and Zamparelli, R. (2014). Semeval-2014 task 1: Evaluation of compositional distributional semantic models on full sentences through semantic relatedness and textual entailment. In *Proceedings of the 8th international workshop on semantic evaluation (SemEval 2014)*, pages 1–8.

McCoy, R. T., Pavlick, E., and Linzen, T. (2019). Right for the wrong reasons: Diagnosing syntactic heuristics in natural language inference. *arXiv preprint arXiv:1902.01007*.

Pires, T., Schlinger, E., and Garrette, D. (2019). How multilingual is multilingual bert? *arXiv preprint arXiv:1906.01502*.

Pratapa, A. and Choudhury, M. (2017). Quantitative characterization of code switching patterns in complex multiparty conversations: A case study on hindi movie scripts. In *Proceedings of the 14th International Conference on Natural Language Processing (ICON-2017)*, pages 75–84.

Pratapa, A., Bhat, G., Choudhury, M., Sitaram, S., Dandapat, S., and Bali, K. (2018). Language modeling for code-mixing: The role of linguistic theory based synthetic data. In *Proceedings of the 56th Annual Meeting of the Association for Computational Linguistics (Volume 1: Long Papers)*, pages 1543–1553.

Rudinger, R., May, C., and Van Durme, B. (2017). Social bias in elicited natural language inferences. In *Proceedings of the First ACL Workshop on Ethics in Natural Language Processing*, pages 74–79.

Talman, A. and Chatzikyriakidis, S. (2018). Testing the generalization power of neural network models across nli benchmarks. *arXiv preprint arXiv:1810.09774*.

Wang, A., Singh, A., Michael, J., Hill, F., Levy, O., and Bowman, S. (2018). Glue: A multi-task benchmark and analysis platform for natural language understanding. In *Proceedings of the 2018 EMNLP Workshop BlackboxNLP: Analyzing and Interpreting Neural Networks for NLP*, pages 353–355.

Wang, A., Pruksachatkun, Y., Nangia, N., Singh, A., Michael, J., Hill, F., Levy, O., and Bowman, S. R. (2019). Superglue: A stickier benchmark for general-purpose language understanding systems. *arXiv preprint arXiv:1905.00537*.

Welleck, S., Weston, J., Szlam, A., and Cho, K. (2018). Dialogue natural language inference. *arXiv preprint arXiv:1811.00671*.

Williams, A., Nangia, N., and Bowman, S. R. (2017). A broad-coverage challenge corpus for sentence understanding through inference. *arXiv preprint arXiv:1704.05426*.

Zhang, C. and Chai, J. Y. (2009). What do we know about conversation participants: Experiments on conversation entailment. In *Proceedings of the SIGDIAL 2009 Conference: The 10th Annual Meeting of the Special Interest Group on Discourse and Dialogue*, pages 206–215. Association for Computational Linguistics.

Zhang, C. and Chai, J. (2010). Towards conversation entailment: An empirical investigation. In *Proceedings of the 2010 Conference on Empirical Methods in Natural Language Processing*, pages 756–766.

Zhang, S., Dinan, E., Urbanek, J., Szlam, A., Kiela, D., and Weston, J. (2018). Personalizing dialogue agents: I have a dog, do you have pets too? In *Proceedings of the 56th Annual Meeting of the Association for Computational Linguistics (Volume 1: Long Papers)*, pages 2204–2213.

When is Multi-task Learning Beneficial for Low-Resource Noisy Code-switched User-generated Algerian Texts?

Wafia Adouane and Jean-Philippe Bernardy
Department of Philosophy, Linguistics and Theory of Science (FLoV),
Centre for Linguistic Theory and Studies in Probability (CLASP), University of Gothenburg
{`wafia.adouane`, `jean-philippe.bernardy`}@gu.se

Abstract

We investigate when is it beneficial to simultaneously learn representations for several tasks, in low-resource settings. For this, we work with noisy user-generated texts in Algerian, a low-resource non-standardised Arabic variety. That is, to mitigate the problem of the data scarcity, we experiment with jointly learning progressively 4 tasks, namely code-switch detection, named entity recognition, spell normalisation and correction, and identifying users' sentiments. The selection of these tasks is motivated by the lack of labelled data for automatic morpho-syntactic or semantic sequence-tagging tasks for Algerian, in contrast to the case of much multi-task learning for NLP. Our empirical results show that multi-task learning is beneficial for some tasks in particular settings, and that the effect of each task on another, the order of the tasks, and the size of the training data of the task with more data do matter. Moreover, the data augmentation that we performed with no external resources has been shown to be beneficial for certain tasks.

Keywords: Algerian Arabic, code-switched user-generated data, multi-task learning, low-resource colloquial languages

1. Introduction

New breakthrough results are continuously achieved for various natural language processing (NLP) tasks, often thanks to the availability of more data and computational power. Likewise, various learning frameworks have been proposed for NLP including multi-task learning. Multi-task learning is about transferring knowledge learned in one task to other tasks by sharing representations (Caruana, 1997). The assumption is that the final learned shared representations are conditioned on the multiple tasks learned simultaneously, and as such they generalise better compared to separate training for each task. This works well when the jointly learned tasks are beneficial for each other, or in cases where a well-performing (auxiliary) task with large data is trained with a related (target) task with less data. However, predicting when tasks are useful for each other remains an open theoretical question and the reported results are still experimental.

This paper is an attempt to take advantage of the state-of-the-art advances in NLP, namely deep neural networks (DNNs) and multi-task learning in order to mitigate the problem of the scarcity of labelled data for colloquial Algerian language (henceforth referred to as ALG). Our main contributions are (1) the creation of a new dataset for code-switched Named Entity Recognition for ALG. (2) An investigation of the settings where it is beneficial to share representations learned between two or several tasks. To this end, we jointly train 4 tasks (or subsets thereof): (1) Code-Switch Detection (CSD), (2) Named Entity Recognition (NER) —both framed as sequence tagging— (3) Spelling Normalisation and Correction (SPELL) —framed as a sequence-to-sequence task— and (4) identifying users' sentiments (SA) —framed as a classification task.

We analyse (1) the effect of each task on another, (2) whether task order matters or not, (3) whether word context for the sequence-to-sequence task is important or not, (4) whether the size of the training data of the task with more data matters, and (5) whether it is useful to augment the training dataset of sequence-to-sequence task (while not requiring any extra resources). We believe that this investigation will extend the utility of multi-task learning in low-resource settings, particularly for code-switched user-generated data. In our experiments we increase the difficulty of the tasks gradually, for instance learning the tasks in pairs, 3 tasks, then 4 tasks, and increase the size of the training data for SPELL progressively.

The paper is organised as follows. In Section 2 we review related work. In Section 3 we describe our tasks and their corresponding datasets. In Section 4 we present the architecture of our model. In Section 5 we describe our experiments and discuss the results. In Section 6 we conclude with the main findings and outline potential directions for future improvements.

2. Related Work

In general, in the context of multi-task learning, the definition of a task is vague: it can refer to an NLP task (Martínez Alonso and Plank, 2017), to a domain (Peng and Dredze, 2017) or to a dataset (Bollmann et al., 2018). Multi-task learning has been applied successfully to a variety of NLP tasks[1] (Collobert and Weston, 2008; Luong et al., 2016; Martínez Alonso and Plank, 2017; Bingel and Søgaard, 2017), focusing on examining the effect of different auxiliary tasks on the performance of a target task. Changpinyo et al. (2018) use joint learning of 11 sequence tagging tasks, investigating whether doing so benefits all of the tasks. Based on the previously reported results, multi-task learning is a promising framework to improve learning with scarce data. Nevertheless, previous work has been mostly limited to morpho-syntactic and semantic sequence labeling tasks, *inter alia*, part-of-speech tagging, syntactic chunking, supersense tagging, semantic trait tagging, semantic role labeling, semantically related words, as well as multi-perspective question answering, and named entity recognition.

---

[1]We cite here only a few examples.

But what about the languages (domains) for which we do not have labelled data for morpho-syntactic and semantic tasks? Unfortunately many languages (or domains like user-generated data) do not have labelled data to perform such tasks. Indeed, NLP research is still focused largely only on a few well-resourced languages, and models are trained primarily on large well-edited standardised monolingual corpora, mainly due to historical reasons or current incentives. Additionally, in many cases the developed techniques fail to generalise (Hovy and Spruit, 2016), even to new domains within a single language (Jørgensen et al., 2015), mostly because they are designed to deal with particularly structured corpora.

Accordingly, it is not clear whether the previously reported results using multi-task learning for NLP generalise to low-resource settings. In this work, we begin to answer this question by applying multi-task learning to user-generated data. As a case study, we take the language used in Algeria (ALG) which uses code-switching, non-standardised orthography as well as it suffers from the lack of any NLP processing tools such as a tokenizer or morpho-syntactic parsers. Like Changpinyo et al. (2018), we examine the settings in which our tasks benefit from multi-task learning, including pairwise tasks, order of the tasks and the size of the training data for the task with more data.

3. Tasks and Datasets

3.1. Tasks

In multilingual societies people have access to many linguistic codes at the same time. In diglossic situations people have access to even different linguistic levels of the same language (Major, 2002). It is the case in North Africa, where for historical reasons many languages and language varieties are used simultaneously to various extents, including mostly Berber, Arabic and French (Sayahi, 2014). These languages and language varieties coexist throughout the region and they are actively used on a daily basis (Rickford, 1990). Consequently in speech-like communications, such as in social media, people tend to mix languages.

- **CSD** the task deals with the detection of the language (in multilingual CSD) or language variety (in diglossic CSD) of each word in its context for disambiguation (Elfardy et al., 2013; Samih and Maier, 2016; Adouane and Dobnik, 2017). This is challenging for ALG, because the same script is used for all languages (MSA, local Arabic varieties, Berber, French, and English). To further complicate matters, vowels are omitted from the text.

- On the other hand, the enormous spelling variations in user-generated data for all languages and language varieties (Eisenstein, 2013; Doyle, 2014; Jørgensen et al., 2015) challenges the standard language ideology with regards to whether human languages are universally standardised and uniform (Milroy, 2001). It also poses serious challenges to the current NLP approaches at all linguistic levels.

- **SPELL** the task aims at reducing orthographic variation and noise in the data, by context-dependent spelling correction and normalisation. Indeed, user-generated content in colloquial languages contains lots of spelling variations because these languages do not have standardised orthography and the content is unedited. We stress that SPELL is different from a usual spelling error correction task in that it deals with a non-standardised code-switched language —there is no existing largely agreed on reference spelling (Adouane et al., 2019).

- **SA** the task deals with identifying users' sentiments from their generated comments.

- **NER** the task deals with the detection and classification of mentions referring to entities into pre-defined classes (person, location, organisation, product, company, etc.).

3.2. Datasets

For each task we use a separate labelled dataset. Table 1 shows statistics about the CSD, SA and NER datasets. We give more details for each dataset below.

CSD		SA		NER	
Class	Total	Class	Total	Class	Total
ALG	118,942	MIX	11,736	OOO	67,7191
MSA	82,114	POS	10,698	PER	7,262
FRC	6,045	NEU	7,262	LOC	4,641
BOR	4,025	NEG	6,424	PRO	3,682
NER	2,283			OTH	901
DIG	1,394			ORG	399
SND	687			COM	248
ENG	254				
BER	99				

Table 1: Statistics about the datasets: CSD (#tokens), SA (#samples) and NER (#mentions).

- **CSD** we use the dataset described by Adouane and Dobnik (2017) which consists of 10,590 user-generated texts labelled at a token level (intrasentential), and includes 9 classes: Local Algerian Arabic (ALG), Berber (BER), French (FRC), English (ENG), Modern Standard Arabic (MSA), and Borrowing (BOR) (which refers to foreign words adapted to the Algerian Arabic morphology), Named Entity as a general class (NER), interjections/sounds (SND) and digits (DIG).

- **SPELL** we use the dataset described in (Adouane et al., 2019) which consists of a parallel corpus with 50,456 words and 26,199 types to be corrected or normalised.

- **SA** we use the dataset described by Adouane et al. (2020) which consists of 36,120 user-generated comments labelled for 4 sentiment classes: positive (POS), negative (NEG), neutral (NEU) and mixed (MIX).

- **NER** we could not get any dataset labelled for NER for ALG that would serve directly our purpose. Therefore we compiled a new dataset by combining the two datasets used for CSD and SA, resulting in 46,710 user-generated comments in total. Then with the help of two other native speakers, we manually labelled it for NER task by classifying every named entity mention in one of the 6 pre-defined classes, following the labelling schema used in OntoNotes Release 5.0 [2]. The classes are: person (PER), location (LOC), product (PRO), organisation (ORG) and company (COM). We tagged the rest of named entity mentions like time and events as "other" (OTH) to distinguish them from non-named entities (OOO). In order to identify multi-word expressions as one named entity chunk, we use the IOB (Inside-Outside-Beginning) labelling scheme. The newly labelled corpus for NER task has 17,133 named entities with IOB details.

4. Models

4.1. CSD and NER

We frame CSD and NER as sequence tagging tasks, i.e., the task is to assign one of the pre-defined tags to each token in an input sequence. We use an encoder-decoder architecture similar the one described by Adouane et al. (2018). However, here the encoders are shared between the tasks, while decoders are task-specific.

- The **Token-level encoder** (in dark orange in Figure 1) encodes the input sequence at the token level. It maps each of 430 possible characters (including special characters and emoticons) to a 100-dimensional representation. It is composed of two convolution layers with 100 features and a filter size of 5 with a dropout rate of 20%, followed by ReLU activation and max pooling in the temporal dimension. In sum, it reads an input sequence character by character and outputs character embeddings for each token (constructs token representations).

- The **Sequence-level encoder** (in light orange) acts at a sequence level. It takes the outputs of the token-level encoder (character embeddings) and outputs word embeddings as a representation for the entire sequence. It consists of two convolution layers with 200 features for the first and 100 for the second, a filter size of 3, ReLU activation and a dropout rate of 5%.

- The **Dense layer** (in dark green for CSD and light blue for NER) with softmax activation maps the output of the sequence-level encoder (word embeddings) to CSD or NER tag sets respectively.

4.2. SPELL

We frame SPELL as a sequence-to-sequence prediction task where the input is a user-generated sequence (text) and the output is its normalised and corrected version (sequence). For this, we use an encoder-decoder architecture (Cho et al., 2014) similar to the one described by Adouane et al. (2019).

- The **Encoder** consists of the shared layers described above in 4.1.

- The **Decoder** (in light green) and consists of one Long Short-Term Memory (LSTM) layer (Hochreiter and Schmidhuber, 1997). It takes the output of the sequence-level encoder (word embeddings) as input and reads it character by character. It has a vocabulary size of 430, 100 units, a token representation size of 100 and a dropout rate of 10%. It is followed by a dense layer (in light green too).

4.3. SA

We frame SA as a text classification task: i.e., assign one of the pre-defined tag sets to an input sequence of any length. We use the model described in (Adouane et al., 2020) which consists of two sub-neural networks.

- The **Encoder** consists of the shared layers described earlier in 4.1, namely the Token-level and the Sequence-level encoders.

- The **Dense layer** (in yellow) with softmax activation maps the output of the sequence-level encoder to SA tags.

All models are trained end-to-end for 50 epochs using a batch size of 64 and Adam optimiser. Gradients with a norm greater than 5 are clipped. As the main focus of the multi-task learning, models share embedding and encoder parameters. Each task is run for a full epoch before switching to the next task. Therefore there is no special code to combine losses (each loss function remains the same for a whole epoch).

5. Experiments and Results

In order to evaluate the performance of our model, we shuffled the datasets and split them (with no overlapping parts) as follows.

For **CSD** we use 30% (3,177 samples) as a test set, 10% (1,059 samples) as a development set, and the remaining 60% (6,354 samples) as a training set.

For **SPELL** we use 20% (37,041 samples) as a test set, 5% (9,261 samples) as a development set, and 75% (138,917 samples) as a training set.

For **SA** we use 17% (6,122 samples) as a test set, 10% (3,612 samples) as a development set, and 73% (26,386 samples) as a training set.

For **NER** we use 30% (14,013 samples) as a test set, 10% (4,671 samples) as a development set, and the remaining 60% (28,026 samples) as a training set.

Note that all datasets are separate and are labelled for different tasks using different tag sets (depending on the task). The hyper-parameters mentioned in Section 4 are fine-tuned on the development sets. Given the small size of the CSD dataset and the high sparsity of the SPELL dataset, after fixing the hyper-parameters, we train both on the training and the development sets, following Yin et al. (2015).

To examine the effect of jointly learning the tasks, we experiment with the following setups:

1. **Pairwise tasks**: To measure the effect of a task on a single other task, we train them two at a time, as shown in Table 2.

---

[2] https://catalog.ldc.upenn.edu/docs/
LDC2013T19/OntoNotes-Release-5.0.pdf

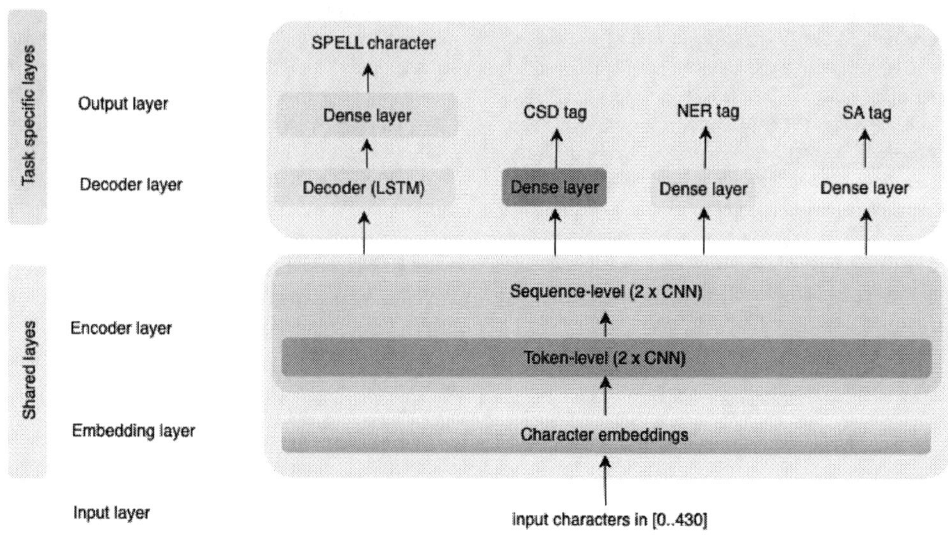

Figure 1: Multi-task model architecture.

2. **Order of tasks**: To check whether the order of tasks affects the overall performance, we run sets of 3 and 4 tasks in various orders. We report the cases where the order has a measurable effect (positive or negative) on the performance.

3. **Context of words**: We are interested in measuring the effect of the context for SPELL (sequence-to-sequence). To do so we either feed the data word by word or whole user-generated text at a time. In the following SPELL will refer to the context-aware task, and SPELL-token refers to the contextless task.

4. **Size of SPELL training data**: We want to investigate the impact of the size of the training data, especially considering that one of the tasks (SPELL) has much more data than the other (CSD, SA and NER) tasks. To do so, we vary only the size of the training data of SPELL while keeping the training sets of CSD, SA and NER fixed each time (as well as the test sets).

5. **Training data augmentation**: We experiment with augmenting the training data for the SPELL task (further referred to as augmented). In this experiment the training data is a combination of tokens and sequence of tokens. (This is equivalent to jointly training SPELL and SPELL-token.)

For each case we take models trained separately (single tasks) as baselines. For **pairwise tasks** we report the detailed results measured as the average Accuracy and macro F-score on the test sets over 50 epochs, thus taking into account the speed of learning. For other experiments (2, 3, 4, and 5) we show the performance, measured as the overall Accuracy, of jointly learning the tasks at hand on the test sets over 20 epochs (we found no significant gain when training for longer and do not report further).

5.1. Pairwise tasks

Task	Tasks	Training	Accuracy (%)	Macro F-score
CSD	CSD	single	96.80	64.54
	CSD + SPELL	joint	96.32	62.27
	CSD + SA	joint	94.30	34.61
	CSD + NER	joint	**97.20**	**71.29**
SPELL	SPELL	single	93.49	
	SPELL + CSD	joint	**93.60**	
	SPELL + SA	joint	93.20	
	SPELL + NER	joint	**93.71**	
SA	SA	single	61.23	54.08
	SA + CSD	joint	**61.35**	53.31
	SA + SPELL	joint	60.74	51.50
	SA + NER	joint	59.82	53.46
NER	NER	single	99.80	49.68
	NER + CSD	joint	**99.82**	48.65
	NER + SPELL	joint	99.78	42.05
	NER + SA	joint	99.74	34.60

Table 2: Macro-average performance of the tasks trained separately and pairwise. Underlined values are baselines. Values in bold show positive effect of jointly learning the tasks at hand.

In Table 2, results measured as Accuracy indicate that learning SPELL, SA and NER tasks jointly with CSD improves their performance over learning them separately — by comparing the performance of single tasks to their performance when jointly trained with CSD.

Note that the gain is mutual between CSD and NER, i.e., jointly learning the tasks benefits both, to different extents. Nevertheless, SPELL and SA slightly benefit from CSD but do not improve it. Interestingly whenever multi-task includes SPELL or SA tasks, the overall performance of the second task (CSD or NER) drops compared to learning the task separately.

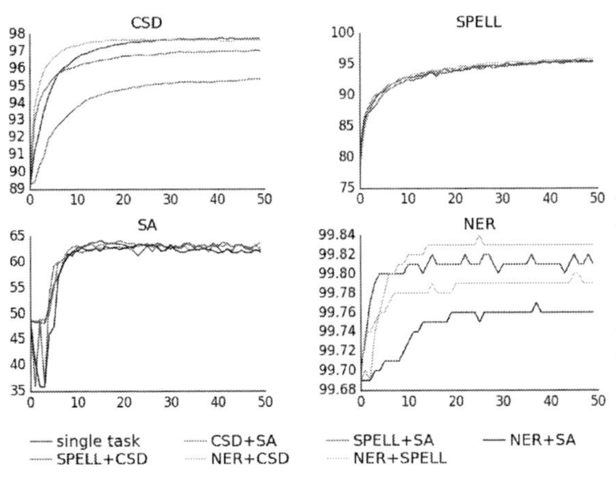

Figure 2: Accuracy (%) of jointly learning 2 tasks for 50 epochs.

A closer look at the results per epoch in Figure 2 indicates that when beneficial, multi-task learning speeds up the performance of the tasks for the first few epochs.

The same behaviour is observed in experiments below (Section 5.2 for instance). This could be because (1) the generated shared representation is not wide enough to capture all tasks perfectly —it needs more parameters in shared layers, or that (2) each task has enough data in itself to reach maximum accuracy. (3) Another hypothesis, which contradicts (2), is that the sparsity and noise in the SPELL and SA training data effects negatively the other tasks.

Jointly training NER with CSD (in turquoise) outperforms training the tasks separately. Furthermore, jointly learning SA with CSD (in red) and SA with SPELL (in pink) outperforms SA trained as a single task. These observations refute hypothesis (2). We controlled for hypothesis (1) by increasing the number of features in the shared layers. That is to say, we tried different values and found that using 500 features in the CNN layers of the token-level encoder, and 500 and 1,000 features for the first and the second CNN layers of the sequence-level encoder has slightly improved the performance of SPELL. However, the overall behaviour of jointly learning SPELL or SA with CSD or NER is still the same. This means that hypothesis (1) does not hold, i.e., it is likely that the noise and sparsity of the SPELL and SA datasets have negative effects on training them jointly with each other or with CSD and NER. Evaluating this hypothesis requires further investigation, which we leave it as future work.

We provide in Table 2 the macro-average F-score for each setting which also reflects the overall impact of jointly learning the tasks by treating all the classes equally. Moreover, since all our datasets are imbalanced both in terms of class distributions and dataset sizes (certain classes have more samples than others and some datasets are much larger than others) we also show the micro F-score at a convergence point for each setting to better analyse the effect of jointly learning the tasks on each class.

Task	Class	CSD	CSD + SPELL	CSD + SA	CSD + NER
CSD	ALG	92.05	89.82↓	83.90↓	91.86↓
	BER	74.29	71.43↓	00.00↓	64.71↓
	BOR	77.10	62.45↓	20.91↓	72.22↓
	DIG	99.93	99.93	99.25↓	99.93
	ENG	26.67	15.38↓	00.00↓	37.50↑
	FRC	83.62	74.45↓	44.93↓	82.17↓
	MSA	90.76	87.88↓	81.71↓	90.39↓
	NER	58.62	26.74↓	02.35↓	62.83↑
	SND	96.14	95.98↓	80.37↓	95.58↓
	Class	**SA**	**SA + CSD**	**SA + SPELL**	**SA + NER**
SA	MIX	60.38	62.48↑	64.20↑	60.70↑
	NEG	41.72	42.44↑	31.88↓	48.21↑
	NEU	53.80	50.95↓	54.95↑	56.11↑
	POS	75.59	75.92↑	76.92↑	75.48↓
	Class	**NER**	**NER + CSD**	**NER + SPELL**	**NER + SA**
NER	COM	21.54	29.55↑	11.32↓	00.00↓
	LOC	80.77	81.50↑	74.03↓	66.05↓
	OOO	99.50	99.59↑	99.45↓	99.42↓
	ORG	09.57	06.67↓	03.87↓	00.00↓
	OTH	26.39	27.41↑	22.66↓	18.75↓
	PER	63.38	69.77↑	54.36↓	52.17↓
	PRO	57.20	59.93↑	54.51↓	47.80↓

Table 3: Micro F-score of the tasks in single and multi-task settings. ↑ marks positive effect and ↓ marks negative effect of jointly learning the 2 tasks at hand.

Results in Table 3 show that jointly training CSD with SPELL or SA has negative effect on all CSD classes (marked with ↓). The negative effect of SA is more pronounced. Minority classes (BER, BOR, ENG, FRC, and NER) are more affected than others. Training CSD with NER has also caused some loss in the performance of some classes of CSD (marked with ↓), but the loss is smaller than when trained with SPELL or SA. The positive effect of NER task on CSD (marked with ↑) could be attributed to its improvements for ENG and NER classes (two minor classes) with a gain of 10.83 and 4.21 points on the F-score respectively. One possible explanation for this improvement could be that the model could extract some underlying structures between some named entity mentions and English words used in the same context. It could be also that it becomes easier for the model to further classify a token in one of NER classes when it knows it is a mention of a named entity.

As shown in Table 3, some classes are harder to learn than others, single trained models struggle also with them. Overall SA benefits from CSD and NER. On the one hand, the gain from CSD could be attributed to its positive effect on MIX, NEG and POS classes. Nevertheless, CSD has a negative effect on NEU with a loss of 2.85 points on the F-score. On the other hand, NER has improved MIX, NEG and NEU classes with a slight loss on POS. SPELL has improved MIX, NEU and POS and caused significant drop on NEG with a loss of 9.84 points on the F-score.

The main difference between the effect of the tasks is mainly on the minority classes (NEG and NEU). This suggests that the tasks could be complementary and their effect could be optimised if trained jointly. This is confirmed when training the 4 tasks together as shown in Figure 4 —at least for the first 10 epochs for SA.

SPELL and especially SA have a significant negative impact on all classes of NER. Nonetheless CSD has improved all NER classes except ORG (which a single NER model struggles to capture, with an F-score of only 9.57).

5.2. Order of tasks

Results in Figure 3 show that, except for NER, jointly learning the CSD, SPELL and SA tasks improves their performance over learning each one separately (as single tasks) only for the first few (7) epochs: after that, learning CSD as a single task outperforms training it with other tasks (blue line), and the effect of learning jointly the tasks is not clear for SPELL and SA.

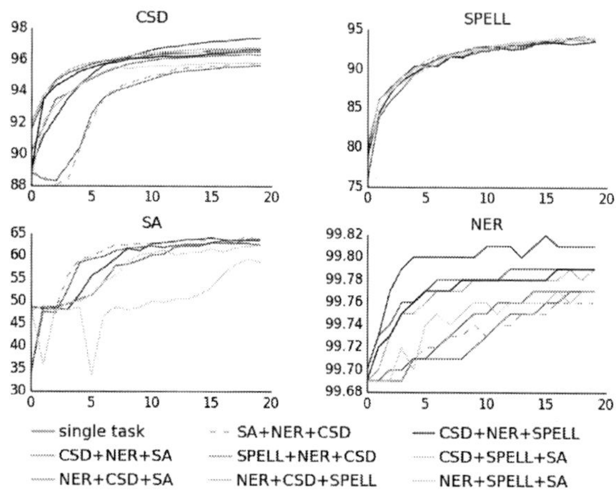

Figure 3: Accuracy (%) of jointly learning 3 tasks for 20 epochs with varying task order.

The results suggest that the order of the tasks has a different effect on the different tasks, for the first few epochs. For instance, while training SA+NER+CSD has a negative effect on both CSD and NER, it has a positive effect on SA (outperforms even SA trained separately). Likewise for CSD-NER-SA but at different extent. NER+CSD+SA has a negative effect on SA and NER overall, but it has a positive effect on CSD at the beginning. This suggests that the order of the tasks affects strongly the first epoch.

The same observation could be applied when jointly learning the 4 tasks as shown in Figure 4. In more details, jointly learning the 4 tasks in NER+CSD+SPELL+SA and SPELL+CSD+NER+SA orders improves SPELL, where the task achieves its best performance. While the same task orders have no positive effect on NER, they do boost the performance of CSD and SA in the beginning but eventually they cause the overall performance to level faster.

5.3. Context of words for SPELL

So far SPELL is trained at a sequence level (as a sequence-to-sequence). In order to measure the effect of the word context we train the same model architecture at a token level, and we refer to it as SPELL-token in Figure 5. The choice of NER+CSD+SPELL+SA order is based on the aforementioned results in Figure 4 where the selected task order performs the best for SPELL (in red). The results indicate clearly that context does matter for SPELL when

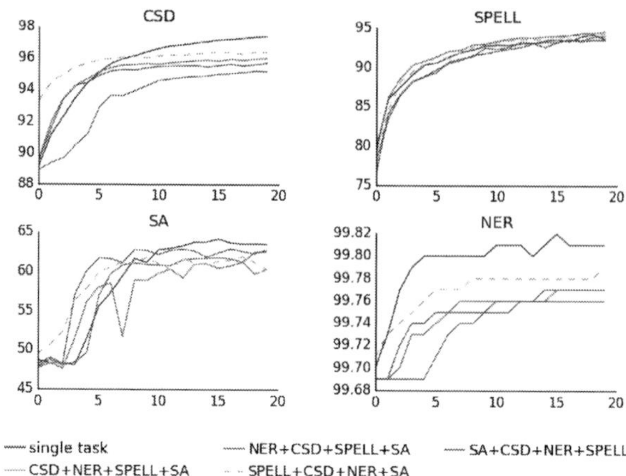

Figure 4: Accuracy (%) of jointly learning 4 tasks for 20 epochs with varying task order.

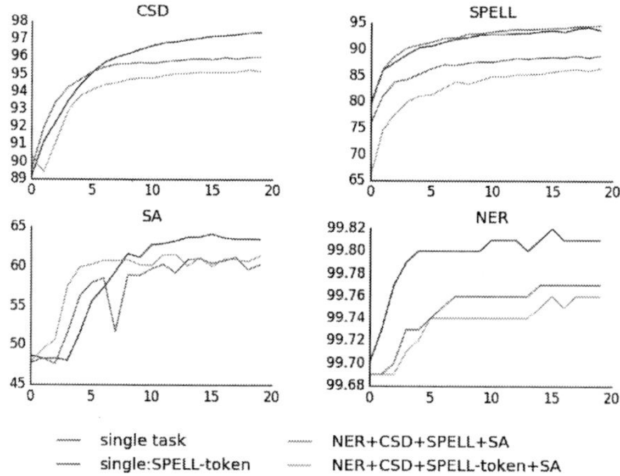

Figure 5: Accuracy (%) of jointly learning 4 tasks with(out) word context for SPELL.

trained separately and for CSD and NER tasks when trained jointly with SPELL and SA. Surprisingly, SPELL (with context) has a positive effect on SA only for the first 6 epochs then the effect is reversed. SPELL-token has an even more positive effect on SA before epoch 8. This suggests that either SA and SPELL datasets could include more ambiguity compared to other datasets, or that the noise of the two datasets hinders learning the tasks jointly.

5.4. Size of SPELL training data

As mentioned earlier, in this experiment we only vary the size of the training set for SPELL. We try 10k, 50k, 100k and all (185k)) and keep the rest unchanged to investigate whether this has any impact on jointly learning the tasks. We use the same task order, namely NER+CSD+SPELL+SA as motivated earlier, and we refer to it as multi-task in Figure 6.

In single task learning, the learning curves of SPELL in Figure 6 indicate that the performance of the task improves quickly with more data (by comparing the performances of

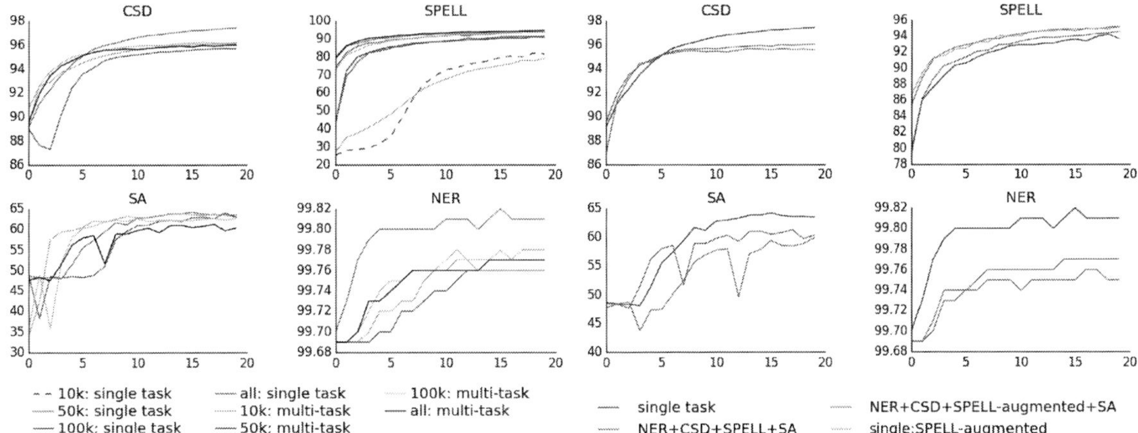

Figure 6: Accuracy (%) of jointly learning 4 tasks with varying SPELL training size. Single task: learning each task separately (baselines). Multi-task: jointly learning the tasks in NER+CSD+SPELL+SA order. All: train on all training sets as described in Section 5.

Figure 7: Accuracy (%) of jointly learning 4 tasks with data augmentation for SPELL. Augmented: using token + sequence as input to SPELL.

100k to 10k and 50k training samples). However, the performance levels with 100k samples, even though it takes a few more epochs to reach the performance than when using all training data. Towards the end the two lines are almost superposed. One possible explanation is that most representative data is already covered in 100k samples (the model has already seen enough data to achieve its maximum performance).

In multi-task learning, the same trend of single task learning is observed for SPELL with a small gain in the performance in the beginning when multi-tasking. Interestingly, as the amount of data increases, the gain of multi-tasking diminishes. For CSD, increasing the training size of SPELL from 10k to 50k has a negative effect, but increasing the size to 100k has boosted the performance of CSD especially in the beginning. The same thing is observed for NER and SA. One possible explanation could be that the datasets of 50k or less are too small and subject to random noise.

The best gain of multi-task for CSD is achieved when trained with only 100k of SPELL. NER and SA, exceeding even single task, benefits the most when trained with only 10k of SPELL. SPELL nevertheless follows the "more data better performance" hypothesis.

5.5. Data augmentation

We replicate the same experiment as in Section 5.3, but instead of comparing the performance of SPELL-token and SPELL separately, we augment the SPELL training data by combining both (token and sequence as input). This allows us to optimise the gain, if any, from the SPELL data.

Results in Figure 7 show that multi-task with the augmented data has arguably very little effect on SPELL compared to the single task in the same setting (the two lines are nearly superposed). However, data augmentation boosts the performance of SPELL compared to non-augmented data and even achieves its best performance. This rejects again hypothesis (2) in Section 5.1 because the performance of

SPELL keeps increasing with more data.

On the one hand, augmenting SPELL data has a notable positive effect on SPELL when jointly trained with the other tasks compared to the same setting with non-augmented data (comparing green and red lines). On the other hand, in terms of effect on the other tasks, while augmenting SPELL data has a negative impact on SA, it offers a small benefit for CSD and NER at the very beginning (before epoch 6), but it is outperformed by the non-augmented data after that.

6. Conclusions and Future Work

We have examined the effect of jointly learning 4 tasks, which are neither morpho-syntactic nor semantic tagging, for noisy user-generated Algerian texts. The main findings of our empirical investigation, which includes a variety of experiments, could be summarised in the following points. (1) Tasks have different impacts on each other when learned jointly. (2) In multi-task learning notable gains are achieved for some tasks when trained jointly with specific tasks. Other tasks benefit from jointly learning them with some other tasks but the gain is only during the first few epochs, especially for tasks with little training data (CSD, NER and SA comparably to SPELL). Training for more epochs degraded their performance compared to learning them separately which is likely caused by the noisiness and sparsity of the data.

This means that it is hard to say whether multi-tasking is useful or not without mentioning several factors such as the tasks themselves, their order, the size of their datasets. (3) Word context for SPELL does matter for the task itself (single task) and for the tasks it is jointly trained with. (4) More SPELL training data does not necessary yield better results neither for the task itself (single task) nor for the tasks it is jointly learned with. In fact, performance is levelling at a certain point, in our case 10k samples for SA and NER, 100k for CSD, confirming this hypothesis. (5) Combining token and sequence level SPELL (augmented) is more beneficial for the task itself (single task) with no gain for multi-task at the convergence point.

In the future, we will examine hypothesis (3) using sequential transfer learning, for instance by running SPELL on all datasets and compare their performances to the non spell corrected and normalised ones. Furthermore, we plan to explore the idea of curriculum learning (Elman, 1993; Hacohen and Weinshall, 2019) on both tasks and individual classes for each task by introducing the tasks or the classes in increasing order of difficulty.

7. Acknowledgements

The research reported in this paper was supported by a grant from the Swedish Research Council (VR project 2014-39) for the establishment of the Centre for Linguistic Theory and Studies in Probability (CLASP) at the University of Gothenburg.

8. Bibliographical References

Adouane, W. and Dobnik, S. (2017). Identification of Languages in Algerian Arabic Multilingual Documents. In *Proceedings of the Third Arabic Natural Language Processing Workshop*, pages 1–8, Valencia, Spain, April. Association for Computational Linguistics (ACL).

Adouane, W., Bernardy, J.-P., and Dobnik, S. (2018). Improving Neural Network Performance by Injecting Background Knowledge: Detecting Code-switching and Borrowing in Algerian texts. In *Proceedings of the Third Workshop on Computational Approaches to Linguistic Code-Switching*, pages 20–28, Melbourne, Australia, July. Association for Computational Linguistics (ACL).

Adouane, W., Bernardy, J.-P., and Dobnik, S. (2019). Normalising Non-standardised Orthography in Algerian Code-switched User-generated Data. In *Proceedings of the 5th Workshop on Noisy User-generated Text (W-NUT 2019)*, pages 131–140, Hong Kong, China, November. Association for Computational Linguistics.

Adouane, W., Touileb, S., and Bernardy, J.-P. (2020). Identifying Sentiments in Algerian Code-switched User-generated Comments. In *Proceedings of the 12th Edition of Language Resources and Evaluation Conference (LREC)–To appear*, Marseille, France, May. European Language Resources Association (ELRA).

Bingel, J. and Søgaard, A. (2017). Identifying Beneficial Task Relations for Multi-task Learning in Deep Neural Networks. In *Proceedings of the 15th Conference of the European Chapter of the Association for Computational Linguistics: Volume 2, Short Papers*, pages 164–169, Valencia, Spain, April. Association for Computational Linguistics (ACL).

Bollmann, M., Søgaard, A., and Bingel, J. (2018). Multi-Task Learning for Historical Text Normalization: Size Matters. In *Proceedings of the Workshop on Deep Learning Approaches for Low-Resource NLP*, pages 19–24, Melbourne, Australia. Association for Computational Linguistics (ACL).

Caruana, R. (1997). Multitask Learning. *Machine Learning*, 28:41–75.

Changpinyo, S., Hu, H., and Sha, F. (2018). Multi-Task Learning for Sequence Tagging: An Empirical Study. In *Proceedings of the 27th International Conference on Computational Linguistics*, pages 2965–2977, Santa Fe, New Mexico, USA, August. Association for Computational Linguistics (ACL).

Cho, K., Van Merriënboer, B., Gulcehre, C., Bahdanau, D., Bougares, F., Schwenk, H., and Bengio, Y. (2014). Learning Phrase Representations using RNN Encoder–Decoder for Statistical Machine Translation. In *Proceedings of the 2014 Conference on Empirical Methods in Natural Language Processing (EMNLP)*, pages 1724–1734, Doha, Qatar, oct. Association for Computational Linguistics (ACL).

Collobert, R. and Weston, J. (2008). A Unified Architecture for Natural Language Processing: Deep Neural Networks with Multitask Learning. In *Proceedings of the 25th International Conference on Machine Learning*, ICML '08, pages 160–167, New York, NY, USA. ACM.

Doyle, G. (2014). Mapping Dialectal Variation by Querying Social Media. In *Proceedings of the 14th Conference of the European Chapter of the Association for Computational Linguistics*, pages 98–106. Association for Computational Linguistics (ACL).

Eisenstein, J. (2013). Phonological Factors in Social Media Writing. In *Proceedings of the Workshop on Language Analysis in Social Media*, pages 11–19, Atlanta.

Elfardy, H., Al-Badrashiny, M., and Diab, M. (2013). Code Switch Point Detection in Arabic. In Elisabeth Métais, et al., editors, *Natural Language Processing and Information Systems*, pages 412–416, Berlin, Heidelberg. Springer Berlin Heidelberg.

Elman, J. (1993). Learning and Development in Neural Networks: the Importance of Starting Small. *Cognition*, 48:71–99, 08.

Hacohen, G. and Weinshall, D. (2019). On The Power of Curriculum Learning in Training Deep Networks. In *Proceedings of the 36th International Conference on Machine Learning, ICML 2019, 9-15 June 2019, Long Beach, California, USA*, pages 2535–2544.

Hochreiter, S. and Schmidhuber, J. (1997). Long Short-Term Memory. *Neural Computation*, 9(8):1735–1780.

Hovy, D. and Spruit, S. L. (2016). The Social Impact of Natural Language Processing. In *Proceedings of the 54th Annual Meeting of the Association for Computational Linguistics (Volume 2: Short Papers)*, pages 591–598, Berlin, Germany, August. Association for Computational Linguistics (ACL).

Jørgensen, A., Hovy, D., and Søgaard, A. (2015). Challenges of Studying and Processing Dialects in Social Media. In *Proceedings of the Workshop on Noisy User-generated Text*, pages 9–18. Association for Computational Linguistics (ACL).

Luong, T., Le, Q. V., Sutskever, I., Vinyals, O., and Kaiser, L. (2016). Multi-task Sequence to Sequence Learning. In *International Conference on Learning Representations (ICLR)*.

Major, R. C. (2002). The Bilingualism Reader. Li Wei (ed.). London: Routledge, 2000. *Studies in Second Language Acquisition*, 24:491 – 493.

Martínez Alonso, H. and Plank, B. (2017). When is Multi-task Learning Effective? Semantic Sequence Prediction under Varying Data Conditions. In *Proceedings of the 15th Conference of the European Chapter of the Association for Computational Linguistics: Volume 1, Long Papers*, pages 44–53, Valencia, Spain, April. Association for Computational Linguistics (ACL).

Milroy, J. (2001). Language Ideologies and the Consequence of Standardization. *Journal of Sociolinguistics*, 5:530 – 555, 11.

Peng, N. and Dredze, M. (2017). Multi-task Domain Adaptation for Sequence Tagging. In *Proceedings of the 2nd Workshop on Representation Learning for NLP*, pages 91–100, Vancouver, Canada, August. Association for Computational Linguistics (ACL).

Rickford, J. (1990). Dialects in Contact. *Language in Society - Oxford and New York: Basil Blackwell, 1986*, 19.

Samih, Y. and Maier, W. (2016). Detecting Code-switching in Moroccan Arabic. In *Proceedings of SocialNLP @ IJCAI-2016*.

Sayahi, L. (2014). *Diglossia and Language Contact: Language Variation and Change in North Africa*. Cambridge Approaches to Language Contact. Cambridge University Press.

Yin, W., Schütze, H., Xiang, B., and Zhou, B. (2015). ABCNN: Attention-Based Convolutional Neural Network for Modeling Sentence Pairs. *Transactions of the Association for Computational Linguistics*, 12.

Proceedings of the LREC 2020 – 4th Workshop on Computational Approaches to Code Switching, pages 26–35
Language Resources and Evaluation Conference (LREC 2020), Marseille, 11–16 May 2020
European Language Resources Association (ELRA), licensed under CC-BY-NC

Evaluating Word Embeddings for Indonesian–English Code-Mixed Text Based on Synthetic Data

Arra'di Nur Rizal and Sara Stymne
Department of Linguistics and Philology
Uppsala University
`Arradinur.Rizal.4511@student.uu.se, sara.stymne@lingfil.uu.se`

Abstract

Code-mixed texts are abundant, especially in social media, and poses a problem for NLP tools, which are typically trained on monolingual corpora. In this paper, we explore and evaluate different types of word embeddings for Indonesian–English code-mixed text. We propose the use of code-mixed embeddings, i.e. embeddings trained on code-mixed text. Because large corpora of code-mixed text are required to train embeddings, we describe a method for synthesizing a code-mixed corpus, grounded in literature and a survey. Using sentiment analysis as a case study, we show that code-mixed embeddings trained on synthesized data are at least as good as cross-lingual embeddings and better than monolingual embeddings.

Keywords: Code-mixed data, word embeddings, synthetic corpora, code-mixed embeddings

1. Introduction

People from around the world are able to connect and exchange information instantly, through the internet and social media. This exchange of information is dominated by the English language (Danet and Herring, 2003; Kramarae, 1999; Poppi, 2014). To prepare Indonesians to go global, the English language has been taught to Indonesian students from elementary school. This exposure to the English language instigates frequent Indonesian–English code-mixing in Indonesia (Brown, 2000, p. 139). This phenomenon is clearly observable in social media not only used by Indonesians but also across languages (Cárdenas-Claros and Isharyanti, 2009; Shafie and Nayan, 2013). Code-mixed text is a challenge for the computational linguistic community, where work based on social media text (Chakma and Das, 2016; Barman et al., 2014) is common. This poses a challenge because most models such as word-embedding models assume the training data is monolingual.

In this paper, we focus on code-mixed Indonesian–English text. Code-mixing has also been referred to as intra-sentential code-switching (Hoffmann, 2014), i.e. the two or more languages are mixed within sentences, not only between sentences. In code-mixed sentences, depending on the language, the word in L1 (e.g. Indonesian) is usually not only replaced with its translation in L2 (e.g. English), but can also be merged with affixes of the L1 (e.g. Indonesian). For instance *"Kita perlu* **revise document***nya"* (*ID: Kita perlu memperbaiki dokumennya*; **EN: We need to revise the document**). In the example, the English word *"revise"* is used instead of the Indonesian word *"memperbaiki"* and the English word *"document"* is merged with the Indonesian suffix *"-nya"*.

There is plenty of research on cross-lingual word-embeddings, which can use either monolingual corpora or parallel corpora to do projection, mapping or alignment (Ruder et al., 2017). In most cases, a set of monolingual embeddings in one language is projected to a set of monolingual embeddings in the other language, or both sets are projected into a shared space. These methods might not be enough to capture intra-sentential code-switched words since cross-lingual embedding tries to merge word representations from two sets of monolingual texts. Mixed words will therefore not be represented in cross-lingual word-embeddings. To address this issue, we suggest that a cross-lingual word embedding model based on code-mixed sentences might be needed. We will call these embeddings code-mixed word embeddings. These word embeddings still cover more than one language like cross-lingual embeddings, but they do so in a setting where the languages are mixed, rather than separate. This has previously been proposed for English–Spanish by Pratapa et al. (2018b).

To train a word embedding model of any type, a large amount of data is needed. Crawling social media does not guarantee that we get balanced corpora of diverse patterns of code-mixed sentences, nor that we get a large enough set of code-mixed sentences. To avoid getting a skewed corpus, we need to be able to control class (code-mixed pattern) distribution in our corpus. One possible method is to synthesize the training corpus By synthesizing a corpus, we will be able to control the class distribution in our data set, and we can easily create a large corpus.

A number of studies has previously proposed methods for synthesizing code-mixed text, using a variety of approaches, based on neural networks (Winata et al., 2019; Chang et al., 2019), linguistic theories (Lee et al., 2019; Pratapa et al., 2018a), or heuristics (Wick et al., 2016). None of these studies have incorporated mixed morphology, which is important in the Indonesian–English setting we are interested in. Our study is using a heuristic approach similar to the work by Wick et al. (2016), which is, however, focused on artificial code-switching involving several languages with the end goal of improving cross-lingual NLP, rather then on mimicking naturally occurring code-mixed data with the end goal of processing code-mixed data.

The main purpose of this study is to evaluate whether code-mixed sentences can be better represented by code-mixed embeddings than by cross-lingual embeddings based on

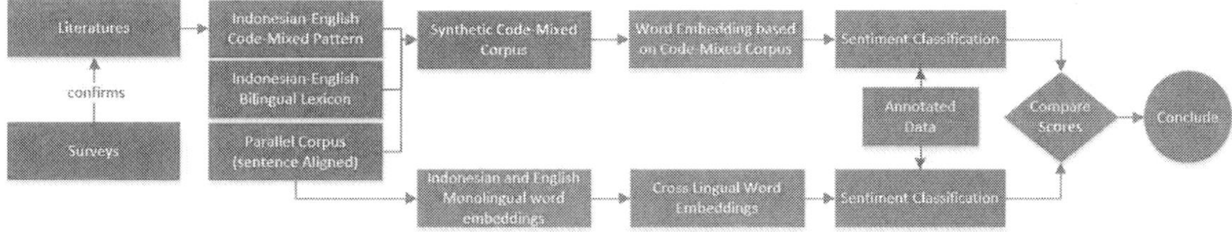

Figure 1: Overview of the methodology for this study. Blue color shows the process of synthesizing a code-mixed corpus. The orange color shows the process of Word Embedding Evaluation

monolingual embeddings. In addition, as a prerequisite task, a method for synthesizing Indonesian-English code-mixed corpus will be presented, grounded in literature and a survey, but simpler than previously proposed methods. The main contributions of this paper are:

- A simple method for creating a synthetic code-mixed corpus of high quality

- Evaluation of code-mixed, cross-lingual and mono-lingual word embeddings on code-mixed Indonesian-English text on a sentiment classification task.

The methodology that we used is shown in Figure 1. The process is divided into two phases. The first one is to synthesize a code-mixed corpus. The second phase is word embedding evaluation, where we compare different types of word embeddings on a sentiment classification task, in order to investigate the feasibility of using word embeddings created from a synthetic code-mixed corpus.

The paper is organized as follows: In section 2 we review related work. In section 3 we describe Indonesian–English code-mixing and section 4 describes the data used. Section 5 describes the synthesis of the code-mixed corpus, including the results on a survey of code-mixed patterns and an evaluation. Section 6 describes how we trained word embeddings, and section 7 gives the results for these word embeddings on a sentiment classification task. The paper ends with a conclusion and suggestions for future work in section 8.

2. Related Work

We are only aware of two attempts to compare monolingual word embeddings, code-mixed word embeddings, and cross-lingual word embeddings trained on corpora with different types of contents. Pratapa et al. (2018b) tested different word embedding techniques on a code-mixed corpus, namely correlation based model, compositional model, and skip-gram model on Spanish–English. They created the bilingual word embedding using monolingual embedding and synthetic code-mixed corpus. They evaluated these word embeddings on a semantic task (sentiment analysis) and a syntactic task (POS tagging). They found that word embeddings created from the code-mixed text, even if it is artificially created, is needed for processing code-mixed text since the existing cross-lingual embeddings are not suitable. Our study is applied to a different language pair,

and we use different methods for training embeddings. We were unable to evaluate on a syntactic task, due to a lack of annotated data for code-mixed Indonesian–English.

Wick et al. (2016) train code-mixed embeddings on synthetic data where five languages are mixed. They evaluate these embeddings on a bilingual analogy tasks and on cross-lingual sentiment analysis. The goal of this work is different from us, since their purpose was to find embeddings that are useful in a cross-lingual learning setting, rather than in a setting where code-mixed data is processed. As for non-synthetically creation of code-mixed corpus, there have been multiple attempts such as Turkish–German Code-Switching Corpus (Çetinoğlu, 2016), Arabic–Moroccan Darija Code-Switched Corpus (Samih and Maier, 2016), Hindi–English Code-Mixed Corpus (Vijay et al., 2018), and English–Spanish Code-Switching Twitter Corpus (Vilares et al., 2016). Yet, English–Indonesian Code-Mixed Corpus does not exist. Most of the code-mixed corpora are created by fetching social media information such as Tweets.

There are several studies that precede our study in code-mixed text synthesis. Some of the recent approach use neural networks. Winata et al. (2019) create a sequence-to-sequence model with a copy mechanism which learn how to combine sentences from parallel corpora to generate code-mixed text. Chang et al. (2019) utilize a generative adversarial network to generate code-mixed sentences.

One early study which synthesizes code-mixed sentences is the work by Wick et al. (2016). They present a method for creating artificially code-switched text across many languages, which they apply to five languages. They use an algorithm where they randomly sample words to be replaced. For each sampled word, they pick one of the concepts, or word senses, possible for that word, and sample a word in any language that belongs to that concept. Our method only mixes two languages, and it is even simpler, in that it does not require a concept dictionary. We also integrate morphology mixing, which is not handled by Wick et al. (2016). Furthermore, the purpose of the two studies are different, since our goal is to mimic naturally occurring code-mixing, whereas their goal is to create data which is useful for cross-lingual learning.

Lately, theories about the nature of code-switched discourse have been used to generate synthetic code-mixed text. Although there is no consensus, there are, among others, three leading theories explaining the formation of code-switched text. They are the Functional Head Constraint (FHC) theory (Di Sciullo et al., 1986; Belazi et al., 1994), the Equivalence Constraint (EC) theory (Sankoff, 1998; Poplack, 1980) and the Matrix Language Frame (MLF) theory (Myers-Scotton, 1997).

One study which uses EC theory to synthesize the code-mixed test is the work by Pratapa et al. (2018a). The basic idea of EC-based code-mixed sentence generation is to ensure that the generated sentence does not break monolingual grammar in both languages. For instance, EC theory will disallow the fragment *book blue* in an English sentence since it is grammatically incorrect. They apply EC-theory to generate synthetic sentences by collapsing two constituency parses tree into one. In order to apply their method, they create a parallel word-aligned corpus that is used to replace every L2 words with L1 words in L2 constituency tree with a corresponding hierarchical structure, on which they can apply the EC-theory to maintain the grammatical structure of L2. In contrast, our study uses a simpler rule-based method replicating the pattern that human produces. It does not need parse trees nor word aligned corpora, but a bilingual dictionary.

Lee et al. (2019) present a study where they use the MLF theory to generate synthetic code-mixed text. MLF theory suggests that in a code-mixed sentence, there will be a dominant language (matrix language) and inserted language (embedded language). This study uses parallel text data aligned at the phrase-level, as a basis for inserting phrases from the embedded language into the matrix language. They apply their method to language modelling, where they sample phrases to insert on the fly, and also combine this with naturally occurring code-mixed data. The idea of using embedded language to create synthetic code-mixed text is similar to our study. An important difference is that their method is based on parallel data whereas our method is based on a bilingual dictionary. They do not model morphology mixing.

There is some work on sentiment classification for code-mixed data. Typical methods are text normalization (Sharma et al., 2015) or adding additional annotations (Vilares et al., 2016).

3. Code Mixing in Indonesian

The Indonesian language has two distinct forms, a formal and an informal variant. Code-mixing can occur with both variants, both in speech and in written format, e.g. magazine articles, text messages, and social media content. Most social media text, such as twitter, use the informal variant. The informal form of Indonesian is mainly categorized into two groups. The first group is the informal usage of words. For instance; the usage of informal pronouns (e.g. *"gue"* instead of *"saya"*; **EN: "I"**), informal abbreviations (e.g. *"lht"* instead of *"lihat"*; **EN: "see"**), and non-standard spelling (e.g. *"haaaaloo"* instead of *"halo"*; **EN: "hello"**). The second group is the informal grammar especially the informal use of affixes. In the informal form, formal affixes are either dropped or replaced. For instance; *"saya menjual ayam"* (**EN: "I am selling chicken"**) becomes *"saya jual ayam"* (the prefix *men-* is dropped) or *"saya ngejual ayam"* (the prefix *"men-"* is replaced with informal prefix

"nge-"). Another example is *"kirimkan paket ini"* (**EN: "send this package"**) becomes *"kirim pake ini"* (suffix -*kan* is dropped) or "kirim*in* paket ini" (suffix *-kan* replaced with informal suffix *-in*). In code-mixed sentences, both categories of informality can be used. For instance; *"Gue nge**update document**"*; *ID: "saya memperbaharui dokumen"*; **EN: "I am updating a document"**. In the example, the formal pronouns *"saya"* is replaced with the informal pronouns *"Gue"* and the informal prefix *"nge-"* is used with english word **"update"** to replace the formal verb *"memperbaharui"*.

Many studies have been conducted to analyze the usage and the form of English–Indonesian code-mixed sentences (Marzona, 2017; Siregar et al., 2014; Kurniawan, 2016; Habib, 2014; Setiawan, 2016). From these studies, we deduced that there are two main forms of Indonesian code-mixed sentences. These two patterns appear in all literature. The first form is word replacement where, for instance, Indonesian nouns, adjectives, verbs, and conjunctions are replaced with their English counterparts. The second form is morphology mixing where Indonesian affixes (formal and informal) are mixed with English verbs. For instance, *"Dokumennya bisa di**download anytime**"* (*ID: Dokumennya bisa diunduh kapan saja*; **EN: The document can be downloaded anytime**). The study by Kurniawan (2016) found that 60 percent of English words in an English–Indonesian code-mixed sentence is the average distribution in code-mixed Indonesian–English text. However, this is based on a small study of only three young persons.

In this work, we will only be concerned with the formal variant, since the formal variant has smaller word variation than the informal variant. Formalizing the corpus helps reduce the Out-of-Vocabulary (OOV) when we do a downstream task such as sentiment analysis. Furthermore, the sentiment analysis corpus (Saputri et al., 2018) we use mostly contains formal Indonesian. However, all methods used would be equally applicable to informal Indonesian.

4. Data and Pre-Processing

We use multiple English–Indonesian sentence-aligned corpora from several genres: The Open Subtitle 2018 Corpus (Lison et al., 2018), TED 2018 Corpus (Cettolo et al., 2012), and GlobalVoice Corpus (Tiedemann, 2012), all taken from the OPUS collection (Tiedemann, 2012). These corpora are cleaned and pre-processed. Table 1 gives an overview of the size of the corpus before and after pre-processing. Open Subtitle 2018 dominates the corpus.

The open subtitle corpus contains a lot of non-letter characters (e.g. ¶\∗#) and formatting (e.g. {\cHFFFFFF}). To clean this, we adjusted the PrepCorpus script[1] to accommodate the Indonesian translation. Moreover, the subtitles also contain song lyrics that are not translated into Indonesian. Therefore, the non-translated sentence pairs were removed from the corpus. These sentences were automatically removed leveraging a bilingual lexicon. A sentence pair is removed if more than 60 percent of the words in the Indonesian sentence are found in the English dictionary. The

---

[1] https://github.com/rbawden/
PrepCorpus-OpenSubs.

Original	TED 2018	Glove	OpenSub	Total
Sentences	117,359	14,448	9,268,181	9,399,988
Tokens – ID	1,646,944	238,968	47,025,227	48,911,139
Tokens – EN	1,882,869	264 689	54,969,761	57,117,319
Cleaned	TED 2018	Glove	OpenSub	Total
Sentences	114,915	14,213	9,237,234	9,366,362
Tokens –ID	1,624,189	232,060	45,943,213	47,799,462
Tokens – EN	1,862,658	257,976	53,723,799	55,844,433

Table 1: The size of corpora before and after pre-processing, for Indonesian (ID) and English (EN).

TED2018 corpus has meta-data information in the corpus. For example <speaker>Al Gore</speaker>. We removed all such meta-data as well as blank lines and double dash characters (--). The Global Voice Corpus contains non-letter characters (e.g. # and ...). These characters as well as blank lines were also removed. After this basic cleaning, we extended all English contractions, (e.g I've → I have) using our script which based on the pycontractions library[2].

Several Indonesian sentences in the corpus were formed in an informal manner. Since this study only concerns formal Indonesian, formalization of the informal sentences was done during the pre-processing. To formalize the informal sentence, we are using the Colloquial Indonesian Lexicon[3] as well as a lexical normalization method from the study by Barik et al. (2019). The lexicon and the normalization method are sufficient for mapping the informal words and affixes back to the standard form. We then lower-cased all data. For English we used Moses (Koehn et al., 2007) to tokenize the data, and for Indonesian, the InaNLP toolkit (Purwarianti et al., 2016). To make sure that the character replacement in Indonesian is consistent with the English Corpus (e.g. apostrophe (') → '), the tokenized corpus was re-tokenized using Moses with the English language as an option. The sentences were not lemmatized because affixes are part of the Indonesian code-mixed pattern.

For synthesizing our code-mixed corpus, and for some of the methods for creating cross-lingual embeddings, as well as for the cleaning described above, we used the bilingual Indonesian–English lexicon from Facebook's ground truth bilingual dictionaries[4]. The bilingual lexicon contains 96,518 words pairs.

5. Synthesizing a Code-Mixed Corpus

In this section, we describe the work on synthesizing the code-mixed corpus. We first describe a survey conducted to investigate the patterns of code-mixing actually in use across Indonesia. We then describe our method for synthesizing and evaluate the resulting corpus.

---

[2] https://github.com/ian-beaver/pycontractions.

[3] https://github.com/nasalsabila/kamus-alay.

[4] https://dl.fbaipublicfiles.com/arrival/dictionaries/id-en.txt.

5.1. Survey

The purpose of the survey is to confirm the code-mixed patterns described in the literature. The goal is to validate whether Indonesian people from different cities would create English–Indonesian code-mixed sentences in the same way. The reason for this is that the literature are typically based on one specific subset of the Indonesian population, e.g. one city (Siregar et al., 2014), one institution (Kurniawan, 2016) or one industry (Marzona, 2017). Therefore, since Indonesian society is not homogeneous, these studies might not represent more than a single variant of Indonesian.

The survey was given out to Polyglot Indonesia members. Polyglot Indonesia is a non-profit organization in Indonesia, which started as a community for language enthusiasts. The organization's members reside across Indonesia.

The survey was made in Google Form which was then spread via Polyglot Indonesia's WhatsApp group, which has 200 members from various cities across Indonesia. Polyglot Indonesia members were chosen because they have linguistic knowledge and they have a diverse cultural and linguistic background. The survey has two questions. 1. The city of origin; 2. Write 10 examples of code-mixed sentences. The survey was conducted for 4 weeks starting in September 2019.

The respondents of the survey (115 people) reside in 14 cities around Indonesia. All of them produced code-mixed sentences with the two patterns that appear in all literature (Marzona, 2017; Siregar et al., 2014; Kurniawan, 2016; Habib, 2014; Setiawan, 2016). For instance "*Harganya ga* **reasonable**" (*ID: Harganya tidak masuk akal*; **EN: The price is not reasonable**) and "*Gue gampang ke***distract** *gitu*" (*ID: saya gampang terganggu*; **EN: I am easily got distracted**). In the two examples, the underlined word is the informal form.

The results of the survey confirm that the code-mixed patterns found in the literature actually reflects the code-mixed patterns used across Indonesia well. The survey also confirms, referring to Matrix Language Frame theory, Indonesian language is the dominant language in Indonesia-English code-mixed text. We thus go on to develop a method implementing the two main patterns: to exchange words and to exchange words with the addition of Indonesian affixes.

5.2. Method for synthesis

We developed an algorithm for the code-mixed sentence synthesizer, based on a monolingual Indonesian corpus and

Algorithm 1 Code-mixed synthesis algorithm

```
 1: for each Indonesian sentences do
 2:     swapped ← 0
 3:     for each word in sentence do
 4:         if swapped / num_words_in_sentence < MAX_SWAP then
 5:             continue with next sentence
 6:         end if
 7:         if random.generate() > SWAP_THRESHOLD then
 8:             strippedWord, affixes ← removeAffixes(word)
 9:             if word in bilingual dictionary then
10:                 swap(word, englishWord)
11:                 swapped++
12:             else if strippedWord in bilingual dictionary then
13:                 mergedWord ← addAffixes(englishWord, affixes)
14:                 swap(word, mergedWord)
15:                 swapped++
16:             end if
17:         end if
18:     end for
19: end for
```

a bilingual dictionary. The reason for basing the synthesis on the Indonesian side is that code-mixed Indonesian–English tend to follow Indonesian syntax. Only formal Indonesian was addressed, but the algorithm can easily be extended to cover informal Indonesian as well.

Algorithm 1 shows how we synthesize the code-mixed corpus. For each sentence, we go through the words in the sentence from left-to-right. For each word, we try to exchange it with a probability set by SWAP_THRESHOLD. If the Indonesian word is found in the bilingual lexicon, it is exchanged (swapped) with the English word, otherwise, we try to strip it of its affixes, and lookup the stem. If the stem is found, we merge the affixes to the English stem, and exchange this mixed word with the original word. Otherwise, no exchange takes place. We limit the number of words exchanged in any sentence to MAX_SWAP. The list of affixes is based on the Indonesian affixes description from the study by Adriani et al. (2007) (section 2). It contains 30 affixes of the following types:

- Inflectional suffixes, for example, "-kah", "-lah", "-tah", "-pun", "-ku", "-mu", and "-nya",

- Derivational prefixes, for example, "be-", "di-", "ke-", "me-", "pe-", "se-", and "te-",

- Derivational suffixes, for example, "-i", "-kan", "-an"

- Derivational confixes, for example, "be-an", "me-i", "me-kan", "di-i", "ke-an".

In our experiments we set SWAP_THRESHOLD to 50% and MAX_SWAP to 60% which is the average percentage of English words used in a code-mixed sentence in the study of Kurniawan (2016). It is also close to the average value in the code-mixed sentences in the corpus taken from the survey result, which is 55.1%. Other values for these two parameters are possible, but we leave the investigation of this effect to future work. The generated code-mixed corpus has the same size as our parallel corpus, over 9M

sentences and 47M words. Some examples are shown in Table 2.

5.3. Corpus Evaluation

To measure the similarity between the real code-mixed sentences and the synthetic code-mixed text, we use two previously proposed measurements: Switch-Point Fraction (SPF) and Code Mixing Index (CMI). SPF (Pratapa et al., 2018a) measures the number of switch-points in a sentence divided by the total number of word boundaries . We define "switch-point" as a point in a sentence at which the words switch to another language. CMI (Gambäck and Das, 2014) measures the number of switches at the utterance level. It is computed by determining the dominant language (the most frequent language) and then counting the frequency of words belonging to the embedded language. We calculate SPF and CMI at the corpus level, averaging the SPF and CMI for all sentences in a corpus.

We used these two measures to investigate if the synthesized corpus seemed to have the same characteristics as a naturally occurring code-mixed corpus. As a point of comparison, we used the corpus produced from the survey. Table 3 shows that the natural and synthesized corpora have very similar values for both measurements, indicating that the distribution of words in the code-mixed corpus mimics that of naturally occurring code-mixed sentences. It also indicates that the choices for the tunable values of the synthesizing algorithm were well chosen.

To further make sure that the generated sentences are good examples of code-mixed text, we conducted a human evaluation. Two native Indonesian bilinguals (Indonesian and English) evaluated 500 generated sentences, chosen at random. 86 percent of the evaluated sentences were considered to be acceptable code-mixed sentences while 14 percent of the sentences were considered to be incorrect, e.g phrases were not translated properly, or not properly formed (e.g. misspelling), or words had translations that are incorrect in that context. For example, the phrase

Good Conversion.		
1	ID: Dia paham betul kisah Irak, mungkin melebihi siapapun.	
	EN: He knows the story of Iraq perhaps more than anybody else	
	CM: Dia paham betul story iraq, probably melebihi anyone .	
2	ID: Anda harus meninggalkan misi ini.	
	EN: You have to leave this mission.	
	CM: Anda harus leaving misi ini.	
3	ID: Foto oleh Forum Pengada Layanan.	
	EN: Photo by Forum Pengada Layanan.	
	CM: Photo by Forum Pengada Layanan.	
4	ID: Dua belas dari pemerkosanya diduga kini telah ditangkap, tapi dua lagi masih buron.	
	EN: Twelve of the suspected rapists have now been arrested, but two are still at large.	
	CM: Dua belas dari rapistnya diduga kini have captured, but two more still buron.	
5	ID: Kesehatannya memburuk sejak kematian putrinya.	
	EN: She is not doing so well since the death of her daughter.	
	CM: Kesehatannya memburuk since deaths daughternya.	
Bad Conversion.		
1	ID: Dia memusnahkan prestasi ekonomi.	
	EN: He destroyed economic achievement.	
	CM: Dia gutted prestasi economy.	
2	ID: Adik saya menjawab Kamu tidak mengerti sama sekali.	
	EN: And my sister replies You do not understand anything.	
	CM: Adik saya answer kamu tidak understand equal once.	
3	ID: Dia mengambil risiko hidup membujang seumur hidup.	
	EN: She risks living the rest of her life alone.	
	CM: Dia retrieving risks alive membujang seumur alive.	

Table 2: Example sentences from the generated synthetic corpus. ID: Indonesian, En: English: CM: Synthesized code-mixed.

Measurement	Survey	Synthetic
SPF	0.2951	0.2989
CMI	0.8559	0.8431

Table 3: Switch-Point Fraction and Code Mixing Index from the corpus taken from survey result and the corpus from synthetic code-mixed text.

"*ID:Terima kasih*" sometime becomes "**EN:accept love**" or "**EN:accept** *ID:kasih*" where it is supposed to be replaced by "**EN:thank you**". To evaluate the inter-evaluator agreement, Cohen's kappa (Cohen, 1960) was used. The kappa coefficient is 0.874 suggesting that both evaluators are in almost perfect agreement (between 0.81 and 1.00) in the evaluation (Landis and Koch, 1977).

Table 2 shows examples of code-mixed sentences judged as good and bad. The main issue with the three bad examples is that word by word translation causes the sentences to be incomprehensible. In example 1, the word "*memusnahkan*" is replaced with the word "*gutted*", which is not contextually correct. This is because the synthesizer does not understand the context of the sentence nor understand word sense. In example 2, the phrase "*sama sekali*" (**EN: "anything"**) is replaced by the fragment "**equal once**". This example shows another example of a phrase that is not translated properly. In example 3, the fragment "*hidup membujang seumur hidup*" which is supposed to be replaced with the fragment "**living the rest of her life alone**" is replaced with the fragment "**alive** *membujang seumur*

alive". In addition, the word "*mengambil*" is supposed to be deleted or not replaced. The conversion for example number three is considered more complex since the synthesizer needs to be able to understand the sentence context and word alignment.

Overall, the majority of issues come from the inability of the synthesizer to replace phrases, which sometimes render sentences unintelligible. Another common issue is the inability to add function words when it is needed. For example, "*ID: ingin tahu*" became "**EN:want know**" where it should became "**EN:want to know**". Misspelling is also a common issue when replacing words and adding affixes. A misspelled word leads to the creation of multiple variants of the same word in the word embedding set, which is not only useless but also reduces the potential embedding quality of the correct word. If the misspelled word were correct, there would be more training data. We think that this issue could be solved with a spelling correction algorithm.

The code-mixed synthesis algorithm is simple, but it can still capture the two types of code-mixed patterns we have identified. As shown, it does overall give good results. There are plenty of options for improvement, though, such as tuning the two thresholds, choosing the words to exchange at random, rather than linearly, and basing the words to exchange on part-of-speech tags. Many of the errors are due to multi-word expressions and collocations, so identifying these, or at least applying the algorithm on the phrase-level could also potentially lead to improvements. Nevertheless, we do believe that the quality of the corpus is good enough for training code-mixed word embeddings.

6. Training Word Embeddings

We first train monolingual embeddings for each language based on each monolingual side of the parallel corpus using FastText[5] (Joulin et al., 2016) with default configuration. The model chosen to create word embeddings is the skip-gram model (Mikolov et al., 2013).[6] The code-mixed word embeddings were created in the same way as the monolingual embeddings, but from the synthetic code-mixed corpus using the same tool (fastText) and configuration as for the monolingual embeddings.[7]

To create cross-lingual word embeddings, we used Vecmap[8] (Artetxe et al., 2018) to combine the Indonesian and English monolingual embeddings into a shared space. We used four different modes provided by Vecmap: supervised, semi-supervised, identical, and unsupervised, with the default configuration. The supervised mode, the semi-supervised mode, and the identical mode are trying to learn how to map two monolingual embeddings to a shared space using seed dictionaries. The difference is on how each mode creates seed dictionaries. The supervised mode uses the full bilingual lexicon of 96,518 word pairs to create a seed dictionary. The semi-supervised mode is intended to be used if there is no large bilingual lexicon. The small number of word pairs will be used to bootstrap the training. In our case, we use the same bilingual lexicon as for the supervised mode to bootstrap the training. The identical mode uses identical words from both sets of monolingual word embeddings to build the seed dictionary. The unsupervised mode does not require a seed dictionary building. Instead, it uses unsupervised initialization based on the isometry assumption of monolingual embeddings. The isometry assumption assumes that the embedding spaces are perfectly isometric.

Since Vecmap is intended to be used for tasks like Machine Translation or zero-shot transfer for a range of tasks, where the texts they are applied to are monolingual, the output of Vecmap are two files (source language and target language). To apply these embeddings to code-mixed data, we need a single set of embeddings. To do this, we added all English words that did not occur in Indonesian to the Indonesian embeddings. This means that word forms that happen to occur in both languages will get the embedding from the Indonesian side. The reason that we prioritized Indonesian for shared words, is that the corpus is syntactically Indonesian. However, other strategies are possible, like averaging the embeddings, but we leave this for future work.

Compared to creating cross-lingual embeddings based on monolingual word embeddings, creating code-mixed word

embeddings is straightforward and a lot faster.[9]

7. Evaluating Word Embeddings

As a final step, we evaluate the different word embeddings on a sentiment classification task. In this section, we describe the sentiment data, the architecture of our sentiment classifier, and the results of the evaluation.

7.1. Sentiment Classification Task

We use the sentiment classification tweets-emotion corpus (5,000 sentences) by Saputri et al. (2018)[10]. We use this corpus because it contains Indonesian–English code-mixed sentences.

For this study, the original code-mixed corpus which has 6 classes (anger, happiness, sadness, fear, love) were converted into two polarities (positive and negative). Anger, sadness, and fear were converted into negative, while happiness and love were converted into positive. The reason for converting the corpus into a binary sentiment task is that it is very small and the classes for the six-way classification had few training examples. The preparation of code-mixed corpus is similar to the Indonesian Corpus. Sentences were formalized, if needed, lower-cased, and tokenized.

7.2. Sentiment Classifier Architectures

Note that the purpose of this study is not to achieve state-of-the-art on sentiment classification, but to compare word embeddings. For that reason, we use a rather simple architecture for classification. In preliminary experiments, we also tried deeper architectures, but they tended to overfit since the data is quite small. To further highlight the strength of each embedding type, the weights of word embeddings were purposely frozen, i.e. not updated, during training.

The classifier architecture used is the Deep Averaging Network architecture by Iyyer et al. (2015) as shown in Figure 2. Each word in the input sentence was converted into its vector representation using word embeddings. Then, from this word representation, a sentence representation was created by averaging the representation of each word. The sentence representation was then fed to multiple fully-connected layers with ReLU activation followed by a softmax layer. A lambda layer was used to create sentence representation. The implementation was done using Keras framework.[11] Cross-entropy was used as a loss function with the Adam optimiser (lr=0.00003, β_1=0.9, β_2=0.999). The training process was done for 20 epochs (the model tends to overfit after 20 epochs) with 32 as batch size. Standard 10-fold cross-validation with a split of 90 percent for the training set and 10 for test set split was used. We used the F1-score as a metric.

7.3. Word Embedding Evaluation Result

Table 4 shows the scores using the different types of word embeddings. The score is the mean and maximum of model

---

[5] https://github.com/facebookresearch/fastText.

[6] According to fasttext documentation, skipgram model is better in performance compared to CBOW in practice.

[7] There was no need to use parallel data for these embeddings, the reason for this was that we wanted the two sets of monolingual embeddings to be comparable. The quality of all these sets of embeddings could be improved by also adding additional monolingual data.

[8] https://github.com/artetxem/vecmap.

[9] 25 minutes compared to 6 hours on an 8 Intel Xeon processor (E5620) with 4 cores @ 2.40Ghz with 192GB RAM

[10] https://github.com/meisaputri21/Indonesian-Twitter-Emotion-Dataset.

[11] https://github.com/keras-team/keras

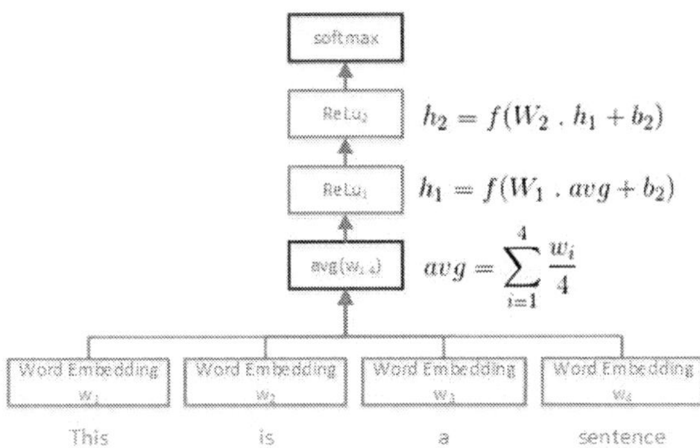

Figure 2: Sentiment Classification Architecture using Deep Averaging Network (Iyyer et al., 2015)

Result in percentage	Mean (STD)	Best
Baseline Embedding		
1 English	62.60 (1.94)	64.77
2 Indonesia	62.87 (2.45)	64.77
Cross Lingual Embedding		
3 Supervised	63.05 (1.60)	66.82
4 Semi-supervised	63.33 (1.49)	65.53
5 Identical	63.17 (1.84)	67.27
6 Unsupervised	63.33 (2.54)	66.36
Code-Mixed Embedding		
7 Code-mixed	63.42 (1.65)	67.27

Table 4: List of sentiment classification cross-validation score employing different embedding

Word Embedding	OOV	Type
Cross-Lingual	6,206	148,737
Code-Mixed	6,406	92,867

Table 5: Number of Out-of-Vocabulary (OOV) on word embedding. The type is the number of distinct word representation in the word embedding used in sentiment classification

F1-score from each fold, accompanied by the standard deviation (STD). Code-mixed embeddings clearly give an advantage compared to using monolingual embeddings, with an average improvement of 0.55% over Indonesian and 0.82% over English. It even gives slightly better results than all of the cross-lingual embedding modes, which requires more processing times and a bilingual lexicon (supervised and semi-supervised). It is also worth noting that the differences between the different types of initialization for the cross-lingual embeddings are minor, showing no advantage of supervision over the unsupervised variants.

Analyzing the word embeddings, we find that the code-mixed word embeddings have a somewhat higher number of OOVs than the cross-lingual embeddings, see Table 5. This is due both to missing English and Indonesian words, which were on one side of the original corpus, but where the English word was never chosen by the swap operation, or the Indonesian word was always swapped. We do note that some words with mixed morphology are covered in the code-mixed embeddings, such as "**driver**nya" (EN: *The driver*) and "**viral**kan" (EN: *make it viral*). In this context, we note that the code-mixed embeddings are actually trained on less data since it is trained on the synthesized Indonesian corpus of 9.4M sentences, whereas the cross-lingual embeddings are trained on 9.4M sentences for each Indonesian and English (18.8M sentences in total), which contributes to this issue. This means that the competitive results on the sentiment analysis task are not due to better coverage of words. We think that the reason code-mixed embeddings give a slightly better score than cross-lingual methods, despite the slightly higher OOV rate and fewer types, is because it has an inherent representation of how both Indonesian and English words are related to each other within the code-mixed context. This feature seems not to be fully captured or replicated by cross-lingual methods.

8. Conclusion and Future work

In this study, we show that code-mixed embeddings are competitive and even slightly better than both monolingual and cross-lingual embeddings on a sentiment analysis task of code-mixed Indonesian–English. A large code-mixed corpus is needed to train these embeddings, but we show that such a corpus can be synthesized based only on a monolingual Indonesian corpus and a bilingual lexicon. We design a simple method for synthesis, which is, however, firmly grounded in both theory and a survey among speakers across Indonesia. The synthesis resulted in 86% acceptable sentences, which we show was enough for training competitive code-mixed embeddings. In this work, we only explored one method for training word embeddings. We think that it would be useful to explore other methods, as well, in order to see how well they work for code-switched data, and to evaluate the embeddings also on other tasks than sentiment analysis. The synthesis method could also be potentially improved in many ways, most importantly by extending the matching from single words to multi-word expressions. Other more resource-intensive options could be to integrate spell checking or a POS-tagger into the synthesis. We also want to further explore the impact of training set size for the different types of embeddings, which might have given an unfair advantage of cross-lingual embeddings in our experiment.

We believe that code-mixed word embeddings have good potential also for other NLP tasks that require cross-lingual word embeddings. If we could use code-mixed word embeddings, the time and cost needed to be spent could be reduced, since code-mixed word embeddings do not require a sentence-aligned corpus or the process to align monolingual word embeddings. It does require either a large code-mixed corpus, or a synthesized corpus, however, as we have shown, good quality code-mixed embeddings can be had also with a simple and resource-lean synthesis method. A further potential advantage of code-mixed embeddings is that they model code-mixed words in the context of both languages, which might be advantageous.

9. Bibliographical References

Adriani, M., Asian, J., Nazief, B., Tahaghoghi, S. M., and Williams, H. E. (2007). Stemming indonesian: A confix-stripping approach. *ACM Transactions on Asian Language Information Processing (TALIP)*, 6(4):1–33.

Artetxe, M., Labaka, G., and Agirre, E. (2018). A robust self-learning method for fully unsupervised cross-lingual mappings of word embeddings. In *Proceedings of the 56th Annual Meeting of the Association for Computational Linguistics (Volume 1: Long Papers)*, pages 789–798.

Barik, A. M., Mahendra, R., and Adriani, M. (2019). Normalization of Indonesian-English code-mixed twitter data. In *Proceedings of the 5th Workshop on Noisy User-generated Text (W-NUT 2019)*, pages 417–424.

Barman, U., Das, A., Wagner, J., and Foster, J. (2014). Code mixing: A challenge for language identification in the language of social media. In *Proceedings of the first workshop on computational approaches to code switching*, pages 13–23.

Belazi, H. M., Rubin, E. J., and Toribio, A. J. (1994). Code switching and x-bar theory: The functional head constraint. *Linguistic inquiry*, pages 221–237.

Brown, H. D. (2000). *Principles of language learning and teaching*. Longman, New York.

Cárdenas-Claros, M. S. and Isharyanti, N. (2009). Code-switching and code-mixing in internet chatting: Between'yes," ya,'and'si'-a case study. *The Jalt Call Journal*, 5(3):67–78.

Çetinoğlu, Ö. (2016). A Turkish-German code-switching corpus. In *Proceedings of the Tenth International Conference on Language Resources and Evaluation (LREC 2016)*, pages 4215–4220.

Cettolo, M., Girardi, C., and Federico, M. (2012). WIT^3: Web inventory of transcribed and translated talks. In *Proceedings of the 16th Conference of the European Association for Machine Translation (EAMT)*, pages 261–268, Trento, Italy, May.

Chakma, K. and Das, A. (2016). Cmir: A corpus for evaluation of code mixed information retrieval of Hindi–English tweets. *Computación y Sistemas*, 20(3):425–434.

Chang, C.-T., Chuang, S.-P., and Lee, H.-Y. (2019). Code-switching sentence generation by generative adversarial networks and its application to data augmentation. In *Twentieth Annual Conference of the International Speech Communication Association (INTERSPEECH)*, pages 554–558. International Speech Communication Association.

Cohen, J. (1960). A coefficient of agreement for nominal scales. *Educational and psychological measurement*, 20(1):37–46.

Danet, B. and Herring, S. C. (2003). Introduction: The multilingual internet. *Journal of Computer-Mediated Communication*, 9(1):JCMC9110.

Di Sciullo, A.-M., Muysken, P., and Singh, R. (1986). Government and code-mixing. *Journal of linguistics*, 22(1):1–24.

Gambäck, B. and Das, A. (2014). On measuring the complexity of code-mixing. In *Proceedings of the 11th International Conference on Natural Language Processing, Goa, India*, pages 1–7.

Habib, S. T. (2014). Code mixing in Twitter among students of English studies 2010 at Universitas Indonesia. In *Makalah Non-Seminar*.

Hoffmann, C. (2014). *Introduction to bilingualism*. Routledge.

Iyyer, M., Manjunatha, V., Boyd-Graber, J., and Daumé III, H. (2015). Deep unordered composition rivals syntactic methods for text classification. In *Proceedings of the 53rd Annual Meeting of the Association for Computational Linguistics and the 7th International Joint Conference on Natural Language Processing (Volume 1: Long Papers)*, pages 1681–1691, Beijing, China, July. Association for Computational Linguistics.

Joulin, A., Grave, E., Bojanowski, P., Douze, M., Jégou, H., and Mikolov, T. (2016). Fasttext. zip: Compressing text classification models. *arXiv preprint arXiv:1612.03651*.

Koehn, P., Hoang, H., Birch, A., Callison-Burch, C., Federico, M., Bertoldi, N., Cowan, B., Shen, W., Moran, C., Zens, R., et al. (2007). Moses: Open source toolkit for statistical machine translation. In *Proceedings of the 45th annual meeting of the association for computational linguistics companion volume proceedings of the demo and poster sessions*, pages 177–180.

Kramarae, C. (1999). The language and nature of the internet: The meaning of global. *New media & society*, 1(1):47–53.

Kurniawan, B. (2016). Code-mixing on Facebook postings by EFL students: A small scale study at an SMP in Tangerang. *Indonesian JELT*, 11(2):169–180.

Landis, J. R. and Koch, G. G. (1977). The measurement of observer agreement for categorical data. *biometrics*, pages 159–174.

Lee, G., Yue, X., and Li, H. (2019). Linguistically motivated parallel data augmentation for code-switch language modeling. In *Twentieth Annual Conference of the International Speech Communication Association (INTERSPEECH)*, pages 3730–3734. International Speech Communication Association.

Lison, P., Tiedemann, J., Kouylekov, M., et al. (2018). OpenSubtitles2018. In *Proceedings of the 11th International Conference on Language Resources and Evaluation (LREC 2018)*. European Language Resources Association (ELRA).

Marzona, Y. (2017). The use of code mixing between Indonesian and English in Indonesian advertisement of Gadis. *Jurnal Ilmiah Langue and Parole*, 1(1):238–248.

Mikolov, T., Chen, K., Corrado, G., and Dean, J. (2013). Efficient estimation of word representations in vector space. *arXiv preprint arXiv:1301.3781*.

Myers-Scotton, C. (1997). *Duelling languages: Grammatical structure in codeswitching*. Oxford University Press.

Poplack, S. (1980). Sometimes I'll start a sentence in Spanish y termino en espanol: toward a typology of code-switching1. *Linguistics*, 18(7-8):581–618.

Poppi, F. (2014). Global interactions in English as a lingua franca. how written communication is changing under the influence of electronic media and new contexts of use. *Ibérica*, 28:225–256.

Pratapa, A., Bhat, G., Choudhury, M., Sitaram, S., Dandapat, S., and Bali, K. (2018a). Language modeling for code-mixing: The role of linguistic theory based synthetic data. In *Proceedings of the 56th Annual Meeting of the Association for Computational Linguistics (Volume 1: Long Papers)*, pages 1543–1553, Melbourne, Australia, July. Association for Computational Linguistics.

Pratapa, A., Choudhury, M., and Sitaram, S. (2018b). Word embeddings for code-mixed language processing. In *Proceedings of the 2018 Conference on Empirical Methods in Natural Language Processing*, pages 3067–3072, Brussels, Belgium, October-November. Association for Computational Linguistics.

Purwarianti, A., Andhika, A., Wicaksono, A. F., Afif, I., and Ferdian, F. (2016). InaNLP: Indonesia natural language processing toolkit, case study: Complaint tweet classification. In *2016 International Conference On Advanced Informatics: Concepts, Theory And Application (ICAICTA)*, pages 1–5. IEEE.

Ruder, S., Vulić, I., and Søgaard, A. (2017). A survey of cross-lingual word embedding models. *arXiv preprint arXiv:1706.04902*.

Samih, Y. and Maier, W. (2016). An Arabic-Moroccan Darija code-switched corpus. In *Proceedings of the Tenth International Conference on Language Resources and Evaluation (LREC 2016)*, pages 4170–4175.

Sankoff, D. (1998). code-switching. *Bilingualism, Language and Cognition*, 50:39–50.

Saputri, M. S., Mahendra, R., and Adriani, M. (2018). Emotion classification on Indonesian twitter dataset. In *2018 International Conference on Asian Language Processing (IALP)*, pages 90–95. IEEE.

Setiawan, D. (2016). English code switching in Indonesian language. *Universal Journal of Educational Research*, 4(7):1545–1552.

Shafie, L. A. and Nayan, S. (2013). Languages, code-switching practice and primary functions of Facebook among university students. *Study in English Language Teaching*, 1(1):187–199.

Sharma, S., Srinivas, P., and Balabantaray, R. C. (2015). Text normalization of code mix and sentiment analysis. In *2015 International Conference on Advances in Computing, Communications and Informatics (ICACCI)*, pages 1468–1473. IEEE.

Siregar, M., Bahri, S., Sanjaya, D., et al. (2014). Code switching and code mixing in Indonesia: Study in sociolinguistics. *English Language and Literature Studies*, 4(1):77–92.

Tiedemann, J. (2012). Parallel data, tools and interfaces in OPUS. In Nicoletta Calzolari (Conference Chair), et al., editors, *Proceedings of the Eight International Conference on Language Resources and Evaluation (LREC'12)*, Istanbul, Turkey, may. European Language Resources Association (ELRA).

Vijay, D., Bohra, A., Singh, V., Akhtar, S. S., and Shrivastava, M. (2018). Corpus creation and emotion prediction for Hindi–English code-mixed social media text. In *Proceedings of the 2018 Conference of the North American Chapter of the Association for Computational Linguistics: Student Research Workshop*, pages 128–135.

Vilares, D., Alonso, M. A., and Gómez-Rodríguez, C. (2016). En-es-cs: An English–Spanish code-switching twitter corpus for multilingual sentiment analysis. In *Proceedings of the Tenth International Conference on Language Resources and Evaluation (LREC 2016)*, pages 4149–4153.

Wick, M., Kanani, P., and Pocock, A. (2016). Minimally-constrained multilingual embeddings via artificial code-switching. In *Thirtieth AAAI Conference on Artificial Intelligence*.

Winata, G. I., Madotto, A., Wu, C.-S., and Fung, P. (2019). Code-switched language models using neural based synthetic data from parallel sentences. In *Proceedings of the 23rd Conference on Computational Natural Language Learning (CoNLL)*, pages 271–280, Hong Kong, China, November. Association for Computational Linguistics.

10. Language Resource References

Tiedemann, J. (2012). *OPUS . . . the open parallel corpus.* http://opus.nlpl.eu/.

Proceedings of the LREC 2020 – 4th Workshop on Computational Approaches to Code Switching, pages 36–44
Language Resources and Evaluation Conference (LREC 2020), Marseille, 11–16 May 2020
European Language Resources Association (ELRA), licensed under CC-BY-NC

Understanding Script-Mixing: A Case Study of Hindi-English Bilingual Twitter Users

Abhishek Srivastava, Kalika Bali, Monojit Choudhury
Microsoft Research, Bangalore, India
{t-absriv, kalikab, monojitc}@microsoft.com

Abstract

In a multi-lingual and multi-script society such as India, many users resort to code-mixing while typing on social media. While code-mixing has received a lot of attention in the past few years, it has mostly been studied within a single-script scenario. In this work, we present a case study of Hindi-English bilingual Twitter users while considering the nuances that come with the intermixing of different scripts. We present a concise analysis of how scripts and languages interact in communities and cultures where code-mixing is rampant and offer certain insights into the findings. Our analysis shows that both intra-sentential and inter-sentential script-mixing are present on Twitter and show different behavior in different contexts. Examples suggest that script can be employed as a tool for emphasizing certain phrases within a sentence or disambiguating the meaning of a word. Script choice can also be an indicator of whether a word is borrowed or not. We present our analysis along with examples that bring out the nuances of the different cases.

Keywords: Mixed-script, Code-mixing, Script-mixing

1. Introduction

Code-switching or code-mixing is a common occurrence in multilingual societies across the world and is well-studied linguistic phenomena (MacSwan (2012) and references therein). Code-switching/mixing refers to the juxtaposition of linguistic units from two or more languages in a single conversation or sometimes even a single utterance.

Despite many recent advancements in NLP, handling code-mixed data is still a challenge. The primary reason being that of data scarcity as it appears very less in formal texts which are usually spread across the World Wide Web. Code-mixing is primarily observed in informal settings like spoken conversations. However, with the advent of social media, it has pervaded to mediums that are set in informal contexts like forums and messaging platforms. Often these platforms are behind privacy walls that prohibit the use or scraping of such data. We resort to Twitter because studies have shown that a large number of bilingual/multilingual users code-mix on the platform (Carter et al., 2013; Solorio et al., 2014; Jurgens et al., 2017; Rijhwani et al., 2017) and the data is easily accessible for analysis.

There are two ways of representing a code-mixed utterance in textual form,

- Entire utterance is written in one script (single-script case)

- It is written in more than one script (mixed-script case)

The second phenomenon is known as script-mixing which occurs when the languages used for code-mixing have different native scripts (such as English-Hindi, French-Arabic, etc). This poses a key challenge for handling code-mixed data collected from social media and other such informal settings. As there is no laid out rule of how someone should write code-mixed sentences, all permutations of scripts can be observed in these sentences. Moreover, script-mixing can introduce noise especially spelling variations occurring

due to transliteration based loosely on the phonetic structure of the words (Singh et al., 2018; Vyas et al., 2014).

The primary contribution of this paper lies in analyzing mixed-script texts present on Twitter and uncovering the underlying patterns as to when and where they are seen. While past studies have thoroughly studied linguistic functions of code-mixing (and language alternation) in speech and text (Poplack, 1980; Woolford, 1983; Alvarez-Cáccamo, 1990; Muysken et al., 2000; Sebba et al., 2012), we examine the functions of *script alternation* in mixed-script text. Our analysis shows that most cases of script-mixing are intentional. We find examples which suggest that script can be used as a tool for emphasizing certain nominal entities[1] within a sentence and also for disambiguating certain words from other close homonyms. We further see how script choice can be used to indicate whether a word is borrowed or not.

The sections are divided in the following manner,

Data Collection: We collect a large corpus from Twitter based on certain meta-information such as the location of the origin of the tweet.

Data Segregation: In order to understand the co-occurrence of code-mixing with script-mixing we tabulate their frequencies among different permutations possible. This gives a clear overview of how the scripts and languages intermix with each other.

Data Analysis: At last, we present a thorough analysis of the patterns found in the mixed-script portion of the corpus when seen under different language contexts.

We complement our analyses with running examples for a better understanding of the different cases. We believe that our study will help understand the nuanced landscape of script-mixing in better detail, and can inspire the development of appropriate NLP tools that can harness mixed-

---

[1]We define nominal entities as phrases that behave either as a noun phrase or a named entity.

language/script data in the future.

2. Related Work

Mixed-script information retrieval deals with cases in which the query and documents are in different scripts. The shared tasks in FIRE 2015 (Sequiera et al., 2015) and FIRE 2016 (Banerjee et al., 2016) present an overview of these approaches. However, they do not work for queries or documents that are in itself represented in the mixed-script text. Jurgens et al. (2014) study the tweets that have code-switched (and possibly mixed-script) hashtags. They observe that authors fluent in non-Latin writing systems often use Latin-transliterated hashtags. In our dataset too, we find examples of tweets that are entirely in Devanagari but for the hashtag, which is in Roman. While the hashtags can be suggestive of certain information such as whether the tweet is spam, an advertisement, or contains sarcasm (Davidov et al., 2010), it could have been added just to insert the post within the global discussion of other posts using the same hashtag (Letierce et al., 2010). Therefore, script alternation using hashtags may not be suggestive of much information and we only analyse the script-mixing that occurs within the grammatical boundary of a sentence.

Bali et al. (2014) analyse English-Hindi code-mixed posts on Facebook to study whether a word is an instance of actual code-mixing or just borrowing. They segregate the code-mixed sentences on the basis of the matrix[2] or embedding language and analyse them individually. However, they only consider the language aspect and limit themselves to Roman sentences.

Our work differs from others because we take the script axis into consideration. We consider all the permutations of script and language and present a rich case study containing qualitative and quantitative analyses. To the best of our knowledge, this is the first study of its kind dealing with code-mixing in a mixed-script scenario.

3. Data Collection and Labelling

3.1. Scraping Tweets

We scrape 1 million tweets from Twitter using TweetScraper[3] which has options to specify certain meta-information such as location and distance range of the scraped tweets.

For an analysis of code-mixing, tweets generated from Indian metropolitan cities are good candidates because the quantity of tweets generated is huge and they also have a better representation of code-mixed tweets. However, since India has a very multilingual[4] population, both the language and the script of the tweets vary widely as per the demography. For example, when we scraped tweets from around Mumbai, we found code-mixing between English and *Marathi* (regional language), and many tweets

---

[2]Code-mixing occurs where one language provides the morpho-syntactic frame into which a second language inserts words and phrases. The former is termed as the *Matrix* while the latter is called *Embedding* (Myers-Scotton, 1993).

[3]https://github.com/jonbakerfish/TweetScraper

[4]There are more than 66 different scripts and 780 written languages in India(Article in The Hindu)

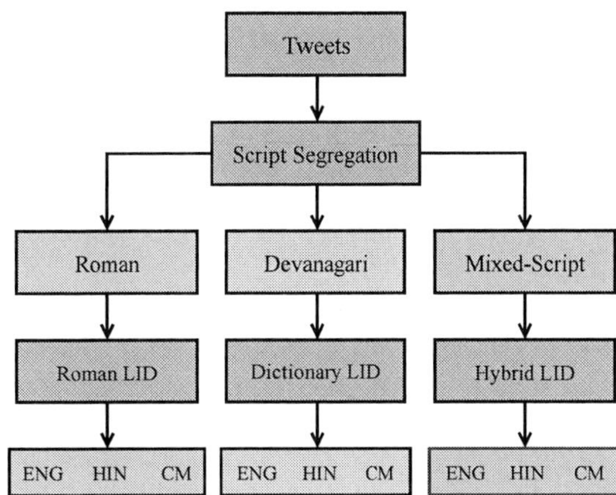

Figure 1: Data collection and labelling.

were written in *Balbodh* script (script for *Marathi*). Similar trends were seen for Bangalore, which had tweets written in *Kannada* script.

In our study, we limit ourselves to Roman and Devanagari, and hence, scrape Tweets from around 200 miles of New Delhi, where Hindi and English are the primary spoken languages. Figure 1 illustrates our approach to data collection and labelling.

3.2. Preprocessing Tweets

We remove the tweets that contain characters in a script other than Roman or Devanagari and then preprocess the rest. We remove the hashtags (#), mentions (@) and hyperlinks using regular expressions. We also de-duplicate the tweets. Eventually, we obtain a dataset of 880,345 tweets.

3.3. Script-Based Segregation

Script-based segregation is a trivial task since each script inherently has a fixed Unicode range. We count the number of words written in Roman and Devanagari for each tweet and then segregate them as follows,

- Tweets written entirely in Devanagari are labelled as *Devanagari*.

- Tweets written entirely in Roman are labelled as *Roman*.

- Tweets that have at least two words from both the scripts are labelled as *mixed-script*.

- Rest of the tweets are dumped as discarded.

Table 1 contains the number of unique tweets in each category after script-segregation. 21,049 tweets are discarded from the dataset.

	Roman	Devanagari	Mixed-script
Tweets Count	617,438	213,113	28,745

Table 1: Tweets after script-based segregation

3.4. Language-Based Segregation

Language-based segregation requires word-level English-Hindi language tags. When dealing with code-mixed sentences, it is a challenge to disambiguate certain transliterated words which share their surface form with a different word (called as homonyms). For example, Table 2 contains the variants of the word 'the' when written in both scripts in different contexts. A robust Language Identification Tool (LID) should be able to handle the following cases,

- For Roman, it must disambiguate between the English word 'the' (दी) and 'the' (थे) which is a Hindi word.

- For Devanagari, it must disambiguate between the English word 'the' (दी) and 'di' (दी) which is a Hindi word.

- For mixed-script, it must disambiguate amongst all these cases.

	English Context	Hindi Context
Devanagari	दी	थे
Roman	the	the

Table 2: Example of homonym ('the')

We are not aware of any LID tool that can simultaneously disambiguate Hindi or English words when written in Devanagari or Roman scripts. Therefore, we undertake different approaches while dealing with different scripts.
For each script, we classify the tweets into three distinct categories,

- English context (EN)
- Hindi context (HI)
- Code-mixed context (CM)

3.4.1. Roman Script

While typing English-Hindi code-mixed text, Roman script is most frequently used (Virga and Khudanpur, 2003; B. et al., 2010), and as a result, there are many LID tools available for it (Gella et al., 2014; Das and Gambäck, 2014; Rijhwani et al., 2017).
We use the LID tool by Gella et al. (2014) and tag all our Roman tweets at word-level. After comparing the count of language tags, we divide the tweets into three categories. Here are a few examples of the tweets,

1. English context (EN)

   (a) Many congratulations on your winning return to competitive tennis super proud
   (b) Congratulations sania that is a super win

2. Hindi context (HI)

   (a) *Pahale to aapko modi ji kaam nahi karne de rahe hai*
   Translation: First of all, Modi-ji is not letting you work.
   (b) *Kya biscuit milna bandh hogaya isko*
   Translation: Has he stopped getting biscuits?

3. Code-mixed context (CM)

   (a) *million hone wala hai dosto* common fast speed *badhawo Tweet karo*
   Translation: Friends, it is going to hit a million; come on! speed up fast; tweet more.
   (b) Good night *dosto ab tumhare hawale ye* trend *sathiyo*
   Translation: Good night, friends! Now the trend depends on you, buddy.

3.4.2. Devanagari Script

Since code-mixing in Devanagari has not been observed frequently in previous works, we expect a majority of the tweets to be in monolingual Hindi. We do not know of any publicly available tool that can perform English-Hindi LID for Devanagari. Therefore, we employ a dictionary-based approach, where we take the list of the most frequent words in English[5] and transliterate them into Devanagari. For Hindi, we generate the dictionary by taking frequent words from a corpus collected from Dainik Jagran[6]. After removing homonyms (such as 'in' and 'the') and wrong transliterations from the dictionaries, we use them to tag the English and Hindi words in the tweets. We further divide the tweets into three language contexts by comparing the count of tags. Here are a few examples of the tweets,

1. English context (EN)

   (a) गुड मॉर्निंग इंडिया
   Translation: Good morning, India.
   (b) ग्रेट लीडर
   Translation: Great leader.

2. Hindi context (HI)

   (a) जन्मदिन की हार्दिक शुभकामनाएं और ढेरो बधाईयां
   Translation: Happy birthday and lots of well wishes.
   (b) क्या तुम सही कर रहे हो?
   Translation: Are you doing the right thing?

3. Code-mixed context (CM)

   (a) आपको फ्रीज करना है तो टेम्परेचर कम करिए
   Translation: Reduce the temperature if you want to freeze.
   (b) गलत लॉजिक
   Translation: Wrong logic.

3.4.3. Mixed-Script

Unlike Roman and Devanagari, a LID tool for mixed-script text has to look at all the possible variations of a word (Table 2). Contextual information about the running language in the sentence is required to predict the language tag of such words. Therefore, even with annotated data, building technology for such a problem is hard.
We end up following a hybrid approach for language tagging mixed-script sentences. We first follow a dictionary-based approach where we language tag the Devanagari

---

[5]https://github.com/first20hours/google-10000-english
[6]https://www.jagran.com/

words as Hindi or English using the approach used in Section 3.4.2.. We then transliterate these Devanagari words into Roman and tag the resulting sentence using the Roman LID tool (Section 3.4.1.). We compare the count of tags generated from the two approaches in each tweet to classify them into one of the three language contexts.

Here are a few examples of the tweets,

1. English Context (EN)

   (a) We should hold up our constitution and provide a relief to all the citizens सत्यमेव जयते
       Translation: We should hold up our constitution and provide a relief to all the citizens *satyamev jayate*[7]. ('Truth alone triumphs')

   (b) नमन I have told you multiple times stay away from them.
       Translation: *Naman*, I have told you multiple times, stay away from them.

2. Hindi Context (HI)

   (a) Dr Santosh ji ka आशीर्वाद प्राप्त हुआ
       Translation: Received the blessings of Dr Santosh

   (b) क्या तुम FB पे हो
       Translation: Are you on FB (Facebook)?

3. Code-Mixed Context (CM)

   (a) I miss you meri behen बहुत दिनों से मैं मिस कर रहा था आपको
       Translation: I miss you my sister; *I was missing you since so many days.*

   (b) वो बाबा ढोंगी नहीं थे so better watch your mouth before blabbering
       Translation: *That Baba (Spiritual Teacher) was not an imposter,* so better watch your mouth before blabbering.

3.5. Data Statistics

After segregating the data along the two axes, we end up with a 3 × 3 table (Table 3) that summarises the intermixing of the two scripts and languages quantitatively. Table 4 contains the numbers as percentages (rounded) for a quick understanding of the scenario. The statistics presented resonate with similar findings of previous works. Liu et al. (2014) observe that non-English tweets are approaching 50% of the total volume of tweets on Twitter. On comparing the frequency of EN context tweets with HI and CM context, the number seems to have already crossed 50% in India.

Bali et al. (2014) observe in a small sample of Indian Facebook posts (in Roman), that as many as 17% of them have code-switching. Our data shows that on Indian Twitter (around New Delhi) 26.5% of the total volume are code-mixed tweets.

Table 5 and Table 6 contain the distribution of unique words across the entire dataset and the mixed-script portion, respectively.

	EN	HI	CM	Total
Roman	357,029	52,401	208,008	617,438
Devanagari	45	212,002	1,066	213,113
Mixed-script	186	10,204	18,355	28,745
Total	357,260	274,607	227,429	859,296

Table 3: Total number of tweets in the entire dataset

	EN	HI	CM	Total
Roman	41.55 %	6.1 %	24.2 %	71.85 %
Devanagari	0.01 %	24.67 %	0.12 %	24.8 %
Mixed-script	0.02 %	1.19 %	2.14 %	3.35 %
Total	41.58 %	31.96 %	26.46 %	100.0 %

Table 4: Percentage of tweets in the entire dataset (rounded)

	EN	HI	CM	Total
Roman	135,817	40,523	156,359	332,699
Devanagari	44	116,775	6,005	122,824
Mixed-script	1,612	27,995	39,576	69,183
Total	137,473	185,293	201,940	524,706

Table 5: Total number of unique words in the entire dataset

	EN	HI	CM	Total
Roman	1,445	5,863	16,784	24,092
Devanagari	168	22,133	22,793	45,094
Total	1,613	27,996	39,577	69,186

Table 6: Total number of unique words in different scripts and language contexts in mixed-script tweets

4. Analysis of Mixed-Script Tweets

After segregating the tweets along the script and language axis, we analyse the mixed-script data. As already discussed in Section 3.4.3., analysing this scenario is non-trivial because contextual information is required. Therefore, we resort to manual annotation and sample 200 tweets each from the Hindi and code-mixed context while taking all the 186 tweets from the English context. We then analyse these tweets separately to find patterns.

If a tweet, which is primarily in one script, contains a short phrase in another script, we refer to that short phrase as an *insertion*.

4.1. English Context

We observe that all the 186 tweets are written primarily in Roman with some Devanagari insertions. We manually go through all the insertions and categorise them (see Table 7). Here are the categories along with examples,

1. **Named Entities**
   We find that 31% of all Devanagari insertions are Named Entities referring mostly to political parties, individual and locations.

Category	Percentage	Examples
Named Entities	31%	नमन, विश्वनाथ, कनॉट प्लेस, कांग्रेसी
Quotes	23%	सत्यमेव जयते, जय श्री राम, भेड़िया आया, सावधान रहे
Hindi Words	35%	ईमानदारी, कंचे, लंगर, नास्तिक, संस्कार
English Words	11%	होल्ड, स्टैंड, हेलो, अमेजिंग

Table 7: Examples of Devanagari insertions within English context (mixed-script case)

(a) Gosh I never knew हरयाणा has so much skull caps wearer a big sign to worry.
Translation: Gosh I never knew *Haryana* has so much skull caps wearer a big sign to worry.

(b) भारतीय जनता पार्टी is the largest democratic party with autocratic designs.
Translation: *Bhartiya Janta Party* is the largest democratic party with autocratic designs.

2. **Quotes**
23% of the insertions are quotes. A few of them are excerpts from Sanskrit *Shlokas*[8] while the others are proper nouns such as the name of a story (e.g. भेड़िया आया - *bhediya aaya*), song, book or slogans (e.g. जय हिन्द - *jai hind*) etc.

(a) Don't let it become the example of भेड़िया आया story pls.
Translation: Don't let it become the example of *Bhediya Aaya* story, please.

(b) अहमस्मि योधः I am a fighter every man has a fighter hidden inside him.
Translation: *Ahamasmi Yoddhah* (Sanskrit Shloka) I am a fighter every man has a fighter hidden inside him.

3. **Hindi Words**
35% of the insertions are Hindi words. Almost all of them are nouns which either do not have a direct translation in English or the translation does not convey the meaning as well as the Hindi word.

(a) I used to have scratch free colorful कंचे of all size it was fun winning it in games.

Translation: I used to have scratch free colorful *Marbles* (toy in India) of all sizes. It was fun winning it in games.

(b) They waited for the अवतार to become king then they behaved as confused and imposed dubious claims.
Translation: They waited for the *incarnation* to become king and then they behaved as confused, and imposed dubious claims.

4. **English Words**
11% of the Devanagari insertions are English words such as *Hello* and *Amazing*. This unexpected occurrence raises many questions such as whether this mixing is intentional or is it just noise. While the other cases make sense, this one does not, primarily because it is not intuitive to have a Devanagari representation of an English word in an overall Roman English sentence.

We have anecdotal evidence that these cases could be due to the predictive keyboards used. Many such keyboards (such as SwiftKey[9]) allow the user to select both Romanized Hindi (often termed as Hinglish) and English as their preferred languages. The keyboard then automatically suggests or replaces Romanized Hindi words into their corresponding Devanagari form. Often such predictions incorrectly convert valid English words to Devanagari as well, leading to such errors.

This specific case requires many such examples to be studied, and hence we leave it aside for future analysis.

(a) अमेजिंग but why not their paid for the safety of passengers vehicles
Translation: *Amazing,* but why are they not paid for the safety of passengers vehicles?

(b) I स्टैंड with Shaheen Bagh.
Translation: I *stand* with Shaheen Bagh.

4.2. Hindi Context

In contrast to the English context, we observe that these tweets are written primarily in Devanagari with Roman insertions. We go through the 200 sampled tweets and manually categorize the insertions (Table 8). Here are the categories along with examples,

1. **Acronyms**
We find that 39.8% of all the Roman insertions in the sample are acronyms. One reason for this occurrence could be the difference in the number of characters required to type an acronym which is higher in Devanagari.

(a) लोगो ने इतने otp मांगे इतने otp मांगे की otp का स्टॉक खत्म हो गया
Translation: People asked for so many OTPs (one time password) that the stock of OTPs ran out.

---

[8] https://en.wikipedia.org/wiki/Shloka

[9] https://www.microsoft.com/en-us/swiftkey

Category	Percentage	Examples
Acronyms	39.8%	CAA, NRC, NPR, BJP, JNU, FB
Named Entities	27.7%	China, Akhilesh, Kejriwal, Smriti
Platform-Specific Terms	4.8%	Follow, Poke, Emoji, Retweet
Frozen Expressions	3.5%	Good morning, via Dainik News
English Phrases	16.4%	Solidarity, Doctorate, Income Tax, Population Control
Hindi Phrases	7.8%	Abe, Dil, Acche Accho

Table 8: Examples of Roman phrases within Hindi context (mixed-script case)

    (b) BJP को वोट दो
    Translation: Vote for BJP.

2. **Named Entities**
27.7% of the insertions are named entities referring mostly to political leaders, political parties, countries and companies.

    (a) रिश्तेदार इतने भी बुरे नही है जितना star plus दिखाता है
    Translation: Relatives are not that bad as portrayed on Star Plus.

    (b) China का सामन खरीदना ही क्यों है
    Translation: Why even buy stuff from China?

3. **Platform-Specific Terms**
4.8% of the Roman insertions are *platform-specific terms* that have their original version in English. We speculate that these terms are in Roman by the virtue of them being used as a nominal entity.

    (a) लोगो को अभी follow back दे रहा हूं आपको बढ़ाने हैं
    Translation: I am following back people, do you want to increase your followers?

    (b) पहले बेटा emoji का प्रयोग करना सीख
    Translation: First, learn how to use the emoji, kid.

4. **Frozen Expressions**
A small portion of the insertions (3.5%) are commonly used frozen expressions in English. Although we expected this number to be higher, the identified phrases capture the overall trend of this category.

    (a) बेवजह दिल पर बोझ ना भारी रखिए जिंदगी एक खूबसूरत जंग है इसे जारी रखिए good morning
    Translation: Don't take too much stress unnecessarily, life is a beautiful battle, keep on fighting it. Good morning.

	Category	Percentage
Natural	Inter-sentential	56%
	Intra-sentential	19%
Cross-script		25%

Table 9: Categories within code-mixed context (mixed-script case)

    (b) रुपए में बिकने के आरोप पर भड़के प्रदर्शनकारी via the hind news
    Translation: On the allegation of being bought in rupees, the Demonstrators flared up. Via The Hind News.

5. **English Phrases**
16.4% of the Roman insertions are English phrases. Almost all of them are noun phrases or words that either do not have a direct translation in Hindi, or the translation is not very popular.

    (a) मुझे वोट नहीं चाहिए ये मोटा भई बस polarization कर के ख़ुश रहता है
    Translation: I don't want votes, the big brother is happy just by polarizing people.

    (b) क्या आप human rights का हवाला देकर उनको छोड़ने की मांग करेगी
    Translation: Will you ask for them to be released for the sake of human rights?

6. **Hindi Phrases**
7.8% of the Roman insertions are Hindi phrases. This unexpected case could again be due to the predictive keyboards as discussed for English insertions (written in Devanagari) in English context in Section 4.1..

    (a) yeh sabka दिल कहता है
    Translation: Everyone's heart says this.

    (b) शायद उसे भी उसके लिए धड़कना अच्छा लगता है kaisi hai kavita
    Translation: Maybe they also like to live for them. How are you, Kavita?

4.3. Code-Mixed Context

Unlike the previous two cases, this context contains tweets that are not in any one primary script. In other words, both the scripts may have an equal proportion in the tweet. We categorize each tweet in the sample into one of the three categories (Table 9).
If the language of a word agrees with the native script it is originally in, it is said to be in *Natural script*, else in *Cross-script*. For example, English words are in *Natural script* when written in Roman and in *Cross-script* when written in Devanagari.

Here are the categories along with some examples,

1. **Natural Inter-Sentential Code-Switching**
Tweets in which script-mixing is at sentence-level and

all the words are in *Natural script* are put in this category. By definition, these tweets would show *inter-sentential* code-switching.

For example, consider these tweets with each sentence having words in *Natural script*,

  (a) thanks good morning a relaxing sunday ahead भारत माता की जय आपका दिन मंगलमय हो
     Translation: thanks good morning a relaxing Sunday ahead *Victory to Mother India, have a fortunate day.*

  (b) क्या होगया यार just chill bro
     Translation: *What happened friend* just chill bro

2. **Natural Intra-Sentential Code-Switching**
Tweets in which script-mixing takes place within the sentence and all the words are in *Natural script* are put in this category. By definition, these tweets would show *intra-sentential* code-switching.

For example, consider these tweets that have mixing within the sentence with words in *Natural script*,

  (a) उनको support करने के लिए आपको कितना money मिला है
     Translation: How much money did you get for supporting them?

  (b) google पर सबसे ज्यादा search होने वाला खिलाड़ी
     Translation: Most searched player on Google.

  (c) oh really देश के students सड़को पर है उनकी कौन सुनेगा
     Translation: Oh, really, the students of our country are on roads. Who will listen to them?

3. **Cross-script**
Code-mixed tweets in which there is at least one word in *Cross-script* are put in this category. In most cases, it appears to be just noise and does not seem intentional. This phenomenon, again, could be due to the predictive keyboards as discussed in Section 4.1. and Section 4.2.

For example, consider these tweets which contain Hindi words in *Cross-script*,

  (a) ji aapke aaj ke DNA pe हमने cigrate <u>kurban</u> कर दी leaved cigarette right now
     Translation: For your today's DNA (News Episode), I sacrificed cigarettes. Left cigarette right now.

  (b) Coffee with karan and pandya <u>yaad hai na</u> next will be manoj tiwari coffee with kejriwal लिख कर ले लो
     Translation: You remember Coffee with Karan and Pandya, right? Next will be Manoj Tiwari's Coffee with Kejriwal.

5. Discussion

5.1. Agreement between Script and Language

In English and Hindi contexts, the insertions mostly have an agreement between the script and the language (the tweets have words that are in *Natural script*). The cases where that is not true are when English words in the English context are written in Devanagari (11%) and Hindi words in the Hindi context are written in Roman (7.8%). As we already discussed, these cases could be due to the predictive keyboards that may erroneously transform a word to a wrong script. In the *Natural script* case, the majority of insertions (named entities, acronyms, etc) are nouns. The cases where they could not be a noun or a noun phrase are quotes (in the English context) and frozen expressions (in Hindi context). However, it should be noted that these phrases are being used as nominal entities. Their identity in these scenarios closely mimics that of a noun phrase.

In code-mixed context, 75% of the tweets are in *Natural script*. However, only 19% of the tweets have Intra-sentential mixing. The rest of the 56% are inter-sentential code-switched tweets. Within these true code-mixed sentences (such as 2 (a) and 2 (b) in Section 4.3.), we observe that if there are short insertions within the sentences, they are mostly nouns.

Overall, it is observed that mostly a mixed-script tweet is in *Natural script* when the insertions are short nouns/noun phrases or nominal entities.

5.2. Script Choice and Borrowing

Script choice can also be an indicator of whether a word is borrowed (a concept introduced by Bali et al. (2014) and later expanded on by Patro et al. (2017)).

As opposed to code-switching, where the switching is intentional and the speaker is aware that the conversation involves multiple languages, a borrowed word loses its original identity and is used as a part of the lexicon of the language (Patro et al., 2017). However, as the authors say, it is very hard to ascertain whether a word is borrowed or not.

We hypothesize that if a word is borrowed from English to Hindi, it will have a higher propensity of being represented in the Devanagari script (as opposed to Roman) in mixed-script tweets in the Hindi context, and vice versa.

For instance, consider these three categories of words,

- Words native to Hindi as a baseline (such as 'Dharma' - धर्म)

- English words that are likely borrowed (such as 'Vote' - वोट and 'Petrol' - पेट्रोल)

- English words that are not likely borrowed (such as 'Minister' - मिनिस्टर)

We measure the propensity of these words being written in Devanagari by calculating the ratio of their frequencies in the two scripts. $P_s(w)$ is the propensity of the word w being written in script s which, in our case, is equal to the frequency of w in s in the mixed-script tweets.

$$\frac{P_{dev}(dharma)}{P_{rom}(dharma)} > \frac{P_{dev}(vote)}{P_{rom}(vote)} > \frac{P_{dev}(minister)}{P_{rom}(minister)}$$

$$236.0 > 7.8 > 0.7$$

The greater the ratio is compared to 1.0, the more likely it is that the word is borrowed from English to Hindi. The ratios for 'vote' (7.8) and 'petrol' (6.0) therefore suggest that they are probably borrowed, whereas 'minister' is not (0.7).

5.3. Script as a Tool for *Emphasis*

In the English context (Section 4.1.), we observe that many Devanagari insertions are used for emphasizing a certain nominal entity within the sentence.

For example,

1. All the nationalist nd most important कट्टर हिन्दू can give me their ids i will follow nd retweet all of ur tweets
   Translation: All the nationalists and most importantly, *staunch Hindus* can give me their IDs and I will follow and retweet all of your tweets

The phrase 'कट्टर हिन्दू' refers to staunch Hindu nationalists. It is used here as a borrowed nominal entity due to the unavailability of a popular English equivalent and has been written in Devanagari for emphasis.

2. I also do not want to be a शिकार of this propaganda movie.
   Translation: I also do not want to be a *prey* of this propaganda movie.

Although there exists a translation equivalent for 'शिकार' ('prey'), the Hindi word is used for an idiomatic effect and is written in Devanagari for stronger emphasis.

3. थू I dont have anything else for you.
   Translation: *Thoo* (Shame), I don't have anything else for you.

This is an interesting example where the Hindi expression for conveying disgust ('थू') has been written in Devanagari. 'थू' has no direct equivalent in English and the closest one ('shame') does not convey the intensity or the idiomatic effect conveyed by it. It has been written in Devanagari for emphasis and also for eliminating any ambiguity since 'थू' in Roman would be written as either 'thu' or 'thoo' which can be mistaken for a misspelling of 'the' or a slang version of 'though'.

Hence, choosing to write a word in a specific script can serve two purposes,

- It can be used to emphasize certain entities.

- It can be used to explicitly disambiguate the sense of certain confusing words.

5.4. Script Inversion for Sarcasm

We also find examples where the native script is inverted for English and Hindi (cross-script representation). The inversion is ironic and is done for adding a dramatic effect to the sarcastic tone.

For example,

1. aree aree द ग्रेट ऑटो कैड ग्यानी
   Translation: Hey, hey, the great Auto-Cad expert.

2. ट्यूबलाइट ye bhi dkh le kabhi gadhe
   Translation: Tubelight (slang for 'fool'), sometimes look at this too, idiot.

6. Conclusion

In this work, we present an analysis of script-mixing for all possible permutations of the scripts (Roman and Devanagari) and languages (Hindi and English) in Twitter. We present a thorough qualitative and quantitative analysis of the mixed-script tweets and discover many patterns that can allow for a rich and concise understanding of the phenomena.

We note that consideration of context is essential when dealing with mixed-script code-mixed sentences. A word-level approach can not capture the complexity of the problem.

It is observed that in most cases, script-mixing is intentional (with the use of acronyms, named entities, quotes, etc) and only in a few cases can it be deemed as noise (such as *Cross-script* tweets). We believe the noise could be due to the predictive keyboards that sometimes erroneously transform a word to a wrong script.

It is interesting to note that the majority of insertions (acronyms, named entities, quotes, phrases, etc) across all the three contexts are either nominal entities themselves or are being used as one. As discussed in Section 5.1., an agreement between script and language mostly exists in cases where the insertions are short nominal entities. Therefore, it can be seen that an agreement exists in a majority of tweets (89% in English Context, 92.2% in Hindi Context and 75% in code-mixed context).

Moreover, script choice can be an indicator of whether a word is borrowed. Examples suggest that a borrowed word from English to Hindi has a higher propensity of being represented in the Devanagari script (as opposed to Roman) in mixed-script tweets in the Hindi context.

We also see how script can be used as a tool for emphasizing nominal entities and for disambiguating word senses explicitly. It is found that certain words are written in their native script regardless of the context for an idiomatic effect (such as 'शिकार' in example 2 of Section 5.3.). We then see examples of how script can be used as a tool for making sarcasm more pronounced.

Our analysis has a wide coverage of the different cases script-mixing can occur in. However, it is limited to the Hindi-English bilingual scenario. Future studies can focus on checking how well this set of analyses generalizes to code-mixing in other languages from other regions in the world such as French-Arabic, Kannada-English, etc.

7. References

Alvarez-Cáccamo, C. (1990). Rethinking Conversational Code-Switching: Codes, Speech varieties, and Contextualization. In *Annual Meeting of the Berkeley Linguistics Society*, volume 16, pages 3–16.

B., S. V., Choudhury, M., Bali, K., Dasgupta, T., and Basu, A. (2010). Resource Creation for Training and Testing of Transliteration Systems for Indian Languages. In *Proceedings of the Seventh International Conference on Language Resources and Evaluation (LREC'10)*, Valletta, Malta, May. European Language Resources Association (ELRA).

Bali, K., Sharma, J., Choudhury, M., and Vyas, Y. (2014). "I am borrowing ya mixing?" An Analysis of English-Hindi Code Mixing in Facebook. In *Proceedings of the*

First Workshop on Computational Approaches to Code Switching, pages 116–126.

Banerjee, S., Chakma, K., Naskar, S. K., Das, A., Rosso, P., Bandyopadhyay, S., and Choudhury, M. (2016). Overview of the Mixed Script Information Retrieval (MSIR) at FIRE-2016. In *Forum for Information Retrieval Evaluation*, pages 39–49. Springer.

Carter, S., Weerkamp, W., and Tsagkias, M. (2013). Microblog language identification: Overcoming the limitations of short, unedited and idiomatic text. *Language Resources and Evaluation*, 47(1):195–215.

Das, A. and Gambäck, B. (2014). Identifying Languages at the Word Level in Code-Mixed Indian Social Media Text. In *Proceedings of the 11th International Conference on Natural Language Processing*, pages 378–387, Goa, India, December. NLP Association of India.

Davidov, D., Tsur, O., and Rappoport, A. (2010). Semi-Supervised Recognition of Sarcastic Sentences in Twitter and Amazon. In *Proceedings of the fourteenth conference on computational natural language learning*, pages 107–116. Association for Computational Linguistics.

Gella, S., Bali, K., and Choudhury, M. (2014). "ye word kis lang ka hai bhai?" Testing the Limits of Word level Language Identification. In *Proceedings of the 11th International Conference on Natural Language Processing*, pages 368–377.

Jurgens, D., Dimitrov, S., and Ruths, D. (2014). Twitter Users #CodeSwitch Hashtags! #MoltoImportante #wow. In Mona T. Diab, et al., editors, *Proceedings of the First Workshop on Computational Approaches to Code Switching@EMNLP 2014, Doha, Qatar, October 25, 2014*, pages 51–61. Association for Computational Linguistics.

Jurgens, D., Tsvetkov, Y., and Jurafsky, D. (2017). Incorporating Dialectal Variability for Socially Equitable Language Identification. In *Proceedings of the 55th Annual Meeting of the Association for Computational Linguistics (Volume 2: Short Papers)*, pages 51–57.

Letierce, J., Passant, A., Breslin, J., and Decker, S. (2010). Understanding how Twitter is used to spread scientific messages.

Liu, Y., Kliman-Silver, C., and Mislove, A. (2014). The Tweets They Are a-Changin': Evolution of Twitter Users and Behavior. In *Eighth International AAAI Conference on Weblogs and Social Media*.

MacSwan, J., (2012). *Code-Switching and Grammatical Theory*, chapter 13, pages 321–350. John Wiley Sons, Ltd.

Muysken, P., Muysken, B., Muysken, P., and Press, C. U. (2000). *Bilingual Speech: A Typology of Code-Mixing*. Cambridge University Press.

Myers-Scotton, C. (1993). Duelling languages. Grammatical structure in Codeswitching–Clarendon Press.

Patro, J., Samanta, B., Singh, S., Mukherjee, P., Choudhury, M., and Mukherjee, A. (2017). Is this word borrowed? An automatic approach to quantify the likeliness of borrowing in social media. *arXiv preprint arXiv:1703.05122*.

Poplack, S. (1980). Sometimes I'll start a sentence in Spanish Y TERMINO EN ESPAÑOL: toward a typology of code-switching. *Linguistics*, 18(7-8):581–618.

Rijhwani, S., Sequiera, R., Choudhury, M., Bali, K., and Maddila, C. S. (2017). Estimating Code-Switching on Twitter with a Novel Generalized Word-Level Language Detection Technique. In *Proceedings of the 55th Annual Meeting of the Association for Computational Linguistics (Volume 1: Long Papers)*, pages 1971–1982.

Sebba, M., Mahootian, S., and Jonsson, C. (2012). *Language Mixing and Code-Switching in Writing: Approaches to Mixed-Language Written Discourse*. Routledge Critical Studies in Multilingualism. Taylor & Francis.

Sequiera, R., Choudhury, M., Gupta, P., Rosso, P., Kumar, S., Banerjee, S., Naskar, S. K., Bandyopadhyay, S., Chittaranjan, G., Das, A., et al. (2015). Overview of FIRE-2015 Shared Task on Mixed Script Information Retrieval.

Singh, R., Choudhary, N., and Shrivastava, M. (2018). Automatic Normalization of Word Variations in Code-Mixed Social Media Text. *CoRR*, abs/1804.00804.

Solorio, T., Blair, E., Maharjan, S., Bethard, S., Diab, M., Ghoneim, M., Hawwari, A., AlGhamdi, F., Hirschberg, J., Chang, A., et al. (2014). Overview for the First Shared Task on Language Identification in Code-Switched Data. In *Proceedings of the First Workshop on Computational Approaches to Code Switching*, pages 62–72.

Virga, P. and Khudanpur, S. (2003). Transliteration of Proper Names in Cross-Lingual Information Retrieval. In *Proceedings of the ACL 2003 workshop on Multilingual and mixed-language named entity recognition-Volume 15*, pages 57–64. Association for Computational Linguistics.

Vyas, Y., Gella, S., Sharma, J., Bali, K., and Choudhury, M. (2014). POS Tagging of English-Hindi Code-Mixed Social Media Content. In *Proceedings of the 2014 Conference on Empirical Methods in Natural Language Processing (EMNLP)*, pages 974–979.

Woolford, E. (1983). Bilingual Code-Switching and Syntactic Theory. *Linguistic inquiry*, 14(3):520–536.

Proceedings of the LREC 2020 – 4th Workshop on Computational Approaches to Code Switching, pages 45–51
Language Resources and Evaluation Conference (LREC 2020), Marseille, 11–16 May 2020
European Language Resources Association (ELRA), licensed under CC-BY-NC

Sentiment Analysis for Hinglish Code-mixed Tweets by means of Cross-lingual Word Embeddings

Pranaydeep Singh and Els Lefever

LT3, Language and Translation Technology Team, Ghent University
Groot-Brittanniëlaan 45, 9000 Ghent, Belgium
pranaydeeps@gmail.com, els.lefever@ugent.be

Abstract

This paper investigates the use of unsupervised cross-lingual embeddings for solving the problem of code-mixed social media text understanding. We specifically investigate the use of these embeddings for a sentiment analysis task for Hinglish Tweets, viz. English combined with (transliterated) Hindi. In a first step, baseline models, initialized with monolingual embeddings obtained from large collections of tweets in English and code-mixed Hinglish, were trained. In a second step, two systems using cross-lingual embeddings were researched, being (1) a supervised classifier and (2) a transfer learning approach trained on English sentiment data and evaluated on code-mixed data. We demonstrate that incorporating cross-lingual embeddings improves the results (F1-score of *0.635* versus a monolingual baseline of *0.616*), without any parallel data required to train the cross-lingual embeddings. In addition, the results show that the cross-lingual embeddings not only improve the results in a fully supervised setting, but they can also be used as a base for distant supervision, by training a sentiment model in one of the source languages and evaluating on the other language projected in the same space. The transfer learning experiments result in an F1-score of *0.556* which is almost on par with the supervised settings and speak to the robustness of the cross-lingual embeddings approach.

Keywords: sentiment analysis, code-mixed text, Hinglish, cross-lingual word embeddings, transfer learning

1. Introduction

Code-mixing is a frequent phenomenon in user-generated content on social media. In linguistics, code-mixing traditionally refers to the embedding of linguistic units (phrases, words, morphemes) into an utterance of another language (Myers-Scotton, 1993). In that sense, it can be distinguished from *code-switching*, which refers to a "juxtaposition within the same speech exchange of passages of speech belonging to two different grammatical systems or subsystems" (Gumperz, 1982), where the alternation usually takes the form of two subsequent sentences. In the proposed research, code-mixing is considered as a phenomenon where linguistic units in Hindi are embedded in English text, or the other way around, but this can take place both at the sentence and word level. As a consequence, we will use the term *code-mixing* as an umbrella term that can imply both linguistic phenomena.

The phenomenon of code-mixing frequently occurs in spoken languages, such as for instance a combination of English with Spanish (so-called *Spanglish*) or English with Hindi (so-called *Hinglish*). More recently, due to the rise of the web 2.0 and the proliferation of user-generated content on the internet, it is increasingly used in written text as well. This social media content is very important to automatically analyse the public opinion on products, politics or events (task of sentiment analysis), to analyse the different emotions of the public triggered by events (task of emotion detection), to observe trends, etc. Code-mixing is, however, very challenging for standard NLP pipelines, which are usually trained on large monolingual resources (e.g. English or Hindi). As a result, these tools cannot cope with code-mixing in the data. In addition, social media language is characterized by informal language use, containing a lot of abbreviations,

spelling mistakes, flooding, emojis, emoticons and wrong grammatical constructions. In the case of Hinglish, an additional challenge is added because people do not only switch between languages (e.g. English and Hindi), but also use English phonetic typing to write Hindi words, instead of using the Devanagari script.

In this paper, we propose a sentiment analysis approach for Hinglish tweets, containing a mix of English and transliterated Hindi. To this end, cross-lingual word embeddings for English and transliterated Hindi are constructed. The proposed research has been carried out in preparation of experiments for the SemEval 2020 shared task on sentiment analysis in code-mixed social media text (Das et al., 2020). This task consists of predicting the sentiment (positive, negative, neutral) of a given code-mixed tweet. Whereas the SemEval task is designed for both English-Hindi and English-Spanish, we will only investigate sentiment analysis for English-Hindi code-mixed tweets in this research.

The remainder of this paper is organized as follows. In Section 2., we summarize relevant related research, whereas Section 3. gives an overview of the data set used to train and evaluate the system. Section 4. describes our approach to sentiment analysis for code-mixed Hinglish data. In section 5., we report on the results and provide an analysis of the performance, while Section 6. concludes this paper and gives directions for future research.

2. Related Research

Related research on computational models for code-mixing is scarce because of the rarity of the phenomenon in conventional text corpora, which makes it hard to apply data-greedy approaches. Previous research, however, has tried to predict code-switching in English-Spanish (Solorio and Liu, 2008a; Solorio and Liu, 2008b) and Turkish-Dutch (Nguyen and Seza Dogruoz, 2013) text corpora. More recently, research has been performed to study code-switching on social media from a computational angle. Vyas et al. (2014) have compiled an annotated corpus for Hindi-English from Facebook forums, and performed experiments for language identification, back-transliteration, normalization and part-of-speech tagging on this corpus. They identify normalisation and transliteration as very challenging problems for Hinglish. Similar work has been carried out by Sharma et al. (2016), who developed a shallow parser for Hindi-English code-mixed social media text. Rijhwani et al. (2017) introduce an unsupervised word-level language detection technique (using a Hidden Markov Model) for code-switched text on Twitter that can be applied to different languages.

Pratapa et al. (2018) compare three bilingual word embedding approaches, bilingual correlation based embeddings (Faruqui and Dyer, 2014), bilingual compositional model (Hermann and Blunsom, 2014) and bilingual Skip-gram (Luong et al., 2015), to perform code-mixed sentiment analysis and Part-of-Speech tagging. In addition, they also train skip gram embeddings on synthetic code-mixed text. Their results show that the applied bilingual embeddings do not perform well, and that multilingual embeddings might be a better solution to process code-mixed text. This is mainly due to the fact that code-mixed text contains particular semantic and syntactic structures that do not occur in the respective monolingual corpora.

Seminal work in sentiment analysis (SA) of Hindi text was done by Joshi et al. (Joshi et al., 2010), who built a system containing a classification, machine translation and sentiment lexicon module. Bakliwal et al. (2012) created a sentiment lexicon for Hindi, and Das and Bandyophadhyay (2010) created the Hindi SentiWordNet. Joshi et al. (2016) introduce a Hindi-English code-mixed dataset for sentiment analysis and propose a system to SA that learns sub-word level representations in LSTM (Long Short-Term Memory) (Subword-LSTM) instead of character- or word-level representations.

Due to the unavailability of NLP tools for Hinglish code-mixed data, we cannot apply a standard sentiment analysis pipeline. To overcome this, we propose a novel method to SA for Hinglish code-mixed tweets that applies cross-lingual word embeddings. To this end, we train monolingual embeddings for code-mixed data using independently gathered Twitter data, and then align the said monolingual embeddings with pre-trained English embeddings. This enables our models to learn from the encapsulated knowledge in pre-trained English embeddings without having much information about the code-mixed structure. Not only does this allow us to build a system that can perform sentiment analysis on bilingual data, but it also enables us to build a transfer learning based system that can derive information from a model trained in one language, to perform predictions in another language.

Most past work building cross-lingual sentiment models does so using translation systems (Zhou et al., 2016) or cross-lingual signals in another form, such as parallel corpora or bilingual dictionaries (Chen et al., 2018). However, since we work with code-mixed (transliterated) Hinglish Twitter data, there are no available resources like parallel corpora or bilingual dictionaries. Moreover, the ever evolving nature of social media text and various spelling alternatives in code-mixed data would make data greedy approaches like parallel corpora redundant.

In the proposed research, we thus build upon the recent research in constructing unsupervised cross-lingual embeddings by exploiting the inherent spacial structural similarity of word embeddings. Mulitple approaches use adversarial learning to learn these mappings with different ideas for optimization. While Zhang et al. (2017) choose to use Earth Mover's Distance as a similarity metric between two embedding spaces, Conneau et al. (2017) opt for the Procrustes solution to refine the mappings. In our experiments, we compare the results obtained when applying (1) the approach of Artexte et al. (2018), which uses Singular Value Decomposition and synthetic bilingual dictionary induction using similarity distributions, and (2) the approach of Conneau et al. (2017). We demonstrate that aligning code-mixed social media text with an anchor language like English helps to increase the performance in both a supervised and transfer learning setting.

3. Data

To train and evaluate our sentiment analysis system for Hinglish, we use the training data provided for the SemEval 2020 shared task on sentiment analysis in code-mixed social media text (Das et al., 2020). This dataset for Hinglish contains 15,131 instances, which have been labeled as positive, negative, or neutral. Besides the sentiment labels, the organisers also provide the language labels at the word level, consisting of the following tags: *en* (English), *hi* (Hindi), *mixed* and *univ* (e.g., symbols, @ mentions, hashtags). Table 1 shows some examples of the Hinglish code-mixed data, whereas Table 2 lists the statistics of the data set used for the sentiment analysis experiments.

As mentioned before, the data set contains a mixture of English and romanized or transliterated Hindi. This produces an additional challenge, as this romanized code-mixed data contains non-standard spellings like *aapke* and *apke* ("your"), non-grammatical constructions like *"Wow the amusement never ends even after the election Daily soap bana ke rakh diya"* which combines an English sentence with a Hindi sentence mid-way, and words which combine an English word with a Hindi alteration like *Jungli* ("wild") and *Filmy* ("glamorous"). Although the data set is tagged with a language label for every word, we did not use this information in our experiments as our aim was to build a common bilingual model that would be applicable for other code-mixed data sets as well.

4. Sentiment Analysis for Hinglish

This research aims to investigate the effectiveness of cross-lingual embeddings to perform sentiment analysis for code-

Tweet	@	Atheist	_	Krishna	JCB	full	trend	me	chal	rahi	hai	Label
Language Tag	Univ	En	Univ	En	En	En	En	En	Hi	Hi	Hi	Positive

Tweet	@	tamashbeen	_	Well	chara	Chor	ke	chele	this	news	is	a	year	old	...	Label
Language tag	Univ	En	Univ	En	Hi	Hi	Hi	En	En	En	En	En	En	En	Univ	Negative

Tweet	@	ur	_	boi	_	kdo	Most	unpractical	and	cool	sword	I	'	ve	seen	Label
Language Tag	Univ	Hi	Univ	Hi	Univ	Hi	En	En	En	En	En	En	Uni	En	En	Neutral

Table 1: Some Examples from the SemEval 2020 Code-Mixed Hinglish Challenge Dataset

Language Labels

English Words	27,594
Hindi Words	28,167
Universal Symbols	2,792

Sentiment Labels

Positive Tweets	5,034
Negative Tweets	4,459
Neutral Tweets	5,683

Table 2: Overview of the statistics of the data set used to perform Hinglish code-mixed sentiment analysis.

mixed data. Since the objective is to demonstrate the viability of cross-lingual embeddings over the simpler, monolingual embeddings, the experimental protocol dictates that the same classifier must be used to evaluate the systems. For the purpose of classification, we opted to use a Bi-LSTM encoder followed by a Softmax layer. Pre-trained crosslingual or monolingual embeddings were fed to the LSTM, the size of the hidden layer was 128 and we incorporated 4 layers in our model. This was followed by a single linear layer and the whole system was trained with Cross-Entropy Loss optimized with Stochastic Gradient Descent (SGD). Each of the models was trained and evaluated with 5-fold cross-validation, and an internal 5-fold cross-validation was performed on the training partition for hyper-parameter optimization.

We investigated two different methods to train our sentiment analysis system for Hinglish code-mixed tweets and compared them with monolingual baseline systems, resulting in the following three experimental setups:

1. Baseline Monolingual Systems: Models exclusively trained using monolingual embeddings

2. Supervised Classification: Models incorporating cross-lingual English-transliterated Hindi embeddings

3. Transfer Learning: Models trained with no supervision on the Hinglish data set but deriving knowledge from the English sentiment data sets

4.1. Baseline Systems with Monolingual Embeddings

Our baseline models were trained with monolingual embeddings in both languages, viz. code-mixed Hindi (Baseline H) and English (Baseline E). To train these monolingual embeddings, we first scraped tweets by means of the

Twitter API in both English and transliterated Hindi. For English 141,566 tweets were scraped, while 252,183 tweets were scraped for Hindi. Hinglish tweets were obtained from the API by querying Hindi tweets and then filtering out tweets containing any Devanagari characters. We were left with 138,589 tweets for Hinglish after removing these 'Devanagari' tweets. Subsequently, monolingual embeddings were trained for both of the above mentioned corpora with a continuous bag-of-words FastText model (Bojanowski et al., 2017), and used to train a bi-directional LSTM (as explained above).

4.2. Supervised Sentiment Analysis with Cross-lingual Embeddings

Cross-lingual embeddings rely on the inherent similarities in language structure and composition to project multiple monolingual embeddings into the same space, enabling tasks which require knowledge of more than one language (Conneau et al., 2018). This kind of embeddings have been used to solve a variety of tasks like word-to-word translation (Chen and Cardie, 2018), evaluating sentence similarity (Bjerva and Östling, 2017) and detecting cognates across languages (Labat and Lefever, 2019). Most methods to project two or more monolingual embeddings into a shared space require a parallel seed dictionary to initialize an alignment which can then be improved upon (Upadhyay et al., 2016). The latter approach is not feasible, though, in this particular setting, as we aim to align English words with code-mixed (transliterated) Hinglish words, which often have no standardised spelling, but on the contrary occur with many variations in social media data. In recent research, however, a number of methods have been explored that seek to create a projection without any seed dictionary by relying on certain basic characteristics of a language in an embedding space. For our experiments, we evaluated two of these methods, namely the Multilingual Unsupervised and Supervised Embeddings (MUSE) Python library[1] and the VecMap toolkit[2], to create cross-lingual embeddings. We selected these methods in particular because of high performance in a number of downstream cross-lingual tasks and the lack of parallel data required to train the cross-lingual embedddings.

The **MUSE** ((Multilingual Unsupervised and Supervised Embeddings) toolkit (Lample and Conneau, 2019) uses a domain-adversarial setting to compensate for the lack of supervision. If the mapping matrix is referred to as W, and the

---

[1]https://ai.facebook.com/tools/muse/
[2]https://github.com/artetxem/vecmap

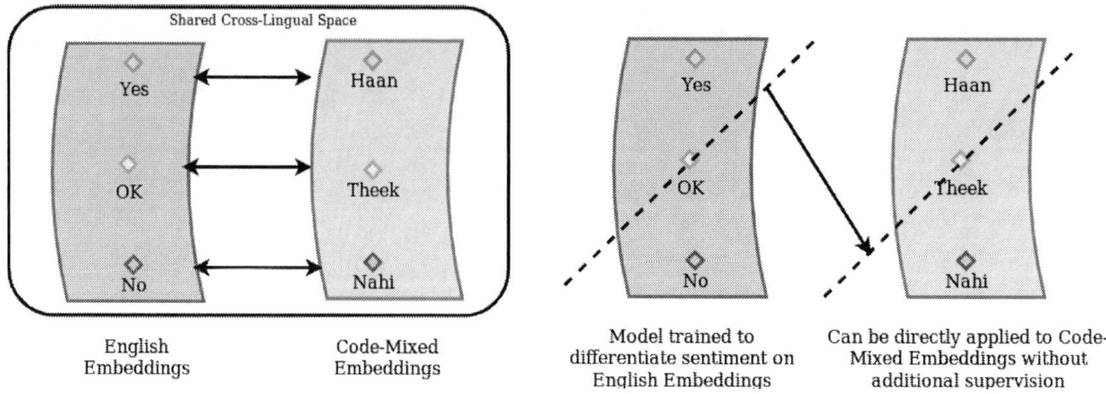

Figure 1: Transfer Learning based Sentiment Analysis for Hinglish, using cross-lingual embeddings

respective monolingual embeddings are referred to as X and Y, then the discriminator is trained to distinguish between WX and Y, whereas W is trained to prevent the discriminator from making accurate predictions by aligning WX and Y as closely as possible. Moreover, an iterative refinement tool using the Procrustes solution is used to further improve the alignment using synthetic dictionaries created from the most frequent words.

The **VecMap** toolkit (Artetxe et al., 2018), on the other hand, starts from the principle that if a similarity matrix of all words in a vocabulary was to be created, then every word would have a unique distribution and that this distribution would be consistent across languages. This principle is used to induct an initial seed dictionary. Optimal orthogonal mappings are then computed using Singular Value Decomposition while iteratively using the improved seed dictionary created by the current mapping. Multiple tweaks to the method, like bi-directional induction of the seed dictionary and symmetric re-weighting of the target language embeddings according to cross-correlation, further improve the quality of the mappings.

For our experiments, we tested two variants of both the VecMap and MUSE cross-lingual embeddings: (1) embeddings aligned with an entirely unsupervised dictionary induction method and (2) embeddings aligned using numerals and common tokens like "https" as a bilingual seed dictionary. This methods is especially interesting to look at as there is a decent overlap between the vocabulary of both embeddings as Hinglish is a derivative of English. The classifiers were then trained and tested by means of 5-fold cross-validation on the SemEval 2020 data.

4.3. Transfer Learning with Cross-lingual Embeddings

Approaches like VecMap and MUSE allow us to find an alignment which transforms monolingual embedddings into a shared space. Since this projection is done with no supervision (or minimal supervision in the case where numerals and identifiers are used as a seed dictionary), it should also be possible to train sentiment models for one of the languages and evaluate them on the other language. This can work if we assume that the model learns

the sentiment-related information in the shared space in which both languages reside. To test these assumptions, we train a bi-directional LSTM on the English sentiment data of the SemEval-2016 "Sentiment Analysis in Twitter" task (Nakov et al., 2016) using English embeddings in the same shared space as code-mixed Hinglish embeddings. We then evaluate the model on the SemEval-2020 Hinglish data set, using the Hinglish embeddings pre-aligned with English embeddings.

Figure 1 illustrates the intuition behind this experiment. Since the model learns to associate particular words to particular sentiments in English during the supervision step, it should ideally also pick up the corresponding words and their sentiments in the code-mixed data due to the shared space, and by consequence be able to perform sentiment analysis with no direct supervision in the code-mixed data. As in the supervised setting (see Section 4.2.), we test for embeddings aligned with VecMap and MUSE, using both (1) the completely unsupervised (*Unsupervised*) and (2) the numerals and special characters seed methods (*SeedDict*).

5. Classification Results

Table 3 gives an overview of the results for supervised sentiment analysis when incorporating monolingual and various flavours of cross-lingual embeddings, while Table 4 shows the results when training a sentiment analysis system on English data (SemEval-2016) and applying it on the code-mixed data set (SemEval-2020). The experimental results for both system architectures reveal a number of interesting outcomes.

Firstly, it can be noted that the SeedDict VecMap approach consistently outperforms other types of cross-lingual embeddings. While for the supervised experiments, the cross-lingual embeddings do not outperform classical embeddings by a large margin, there are small improvements which can be accounted for by the fact that we can use both English as well as code-mixed embeddings to classify a sentence, whereas only one of those can be used at a time in standard monolingual approaches. While the quality of the embeddings may have diminished due to the alignement process, the results are still better due to the increased vocabulary at our disposal.

A tweet like *"One India sabka saath sabka vikas sabka*

	Positive			Negative			Neutral			Macro-Average		
Experiment	Prec	Rec	F-score	Prec	Rec	F-score	Prec	Rec	F-score	Prec	Rec	F-score
English (Baseline E)	0.734	0.574	0.645	0.625	0.633	0.629	0.501	0.595	0.544	0.620	0.600	0.606
Code-Mixed (Baseline H)	0.719	0.620	0.666	0.627	0.656	0.641	0.521	0.566	0.543	0.622	0.614	0.616
MUSE Unsupervised	0.750	0.539	0.627	0.612	0.735	**0.668**	0.511	0.557	0.533	0.624	0.610	0.609
MUSE SeedDict	**0.759**	0.540	0.631	**0.732**	0.528	0.614	0.500	**0.744**	**0.598**	**0.663**	0.604	0.614
VecMap Unsupervised	0.693	**0.691**	0.692	0.570	**0.804**	0.667	**0.565**	0.378	0.453	0.609	0.624	0.604
VecMap SeedDict	0.702	0.684	**0.693**	0.669	0.622	0.645	0.546	0.590	0.567	0.639	**0.632**	**0.635**

Table 3: Precision (Prec), Recall (Rec) and F1-score for all three sentiment classes for the Bidirectional LSTM models trained with various embedding flavours incorporated in a **supervised** system architecture for sentiment analysis for Hinglish.

	Positive			Negative			Neutral			Macro-Average		
Experiment	Prec	Rec	F-score	Prec	Rec	F-score	Prec	Rec	F-score	Prec	Rec	F-score
MUSE Unsupervised	0.570	0.577	0.573	0.523	0.670	0.588	0.428	0.327	0.371	0.507	0.524	0.510
MUSE SeedDict	0.603	0.621	0.612	0.507	**0.789**	0.618	0.449	0.239	0.312	0.519	0.549	0.514
VecMap Unsupervised	0.580	**0.716**	**0.641**	**0.548**	0.688	0.610	0.457	0.268	0.338	0.528	0.557	0.529
VecMap SeedDict	**0.688**	0.529	0.598	0.541	0.748	**0.628**	**0.469**	**0.423**	**0.444**	**0.566**	**0.566**	**0.556**

Table 4: Precision (Prec), Recall (Rec) and F1-score for all three sentiment classes for the **transfer learning** sentiment systems trained on the SemEval-2016 English Twitter Data and evaluated on the SemEval-2020 code-mixed Hinglish Data.

visvas"(One India, with togetherness, progress and trust) is misclassified by the model incorporating monolingual english embeddings as "Neutral" since it cannot pick up the positive code-mixed Hindi words, while a tweet like *"FF Have a great weekend"* is misclassified by the monolingual code-mixed embeddings because of lack of knowledge of English words. Both of these tweets are, however, correctly classified by the VecMap embeddings using a seed dictionary.

It can also be observed that our transfer learning based model is able to perform sentiment analysis with acceptable accuracies without needing code-mixed supervision of any degree. This is a very promising outcome for low(er)-resourced languages, where large dedicated data sets for NLP tasks such as sentiment analysis are lacking. Regarding the baseline approaches, it is also worth noting that the Code-Mixed Baseline does not perform a lot better than the English baseline as one would expect. This can probably be attributed to the quality of the monolingual embeddings, since the English embeddings were trained on the vast Common Crawl data while the Code-Mixed embeddings were trained on a little more than 100,000 scraped tweets. While the classification is understandably accurate for tweets containing a majority of English words like *"Exclusive censor reports of Bharat is world class Words like movie of the year"* and less reliable for sentences predominantly containing code-mixed words like *"YouTube views ko vote samjhne wale agar is bar Nahi jita to Kabhi Nahi jitega"*, the performance could be improved with better alignments and possibly a hybrid approach with minimal supervision.

6. Conclusion

This paper presents various approaches to sentiment analysis for Hinglish code-mixed tweets. Two different system architectures were researched: a supervised classification model incorporating cross-lingual embeddings for English-transliterated Hindi data and a transfer learning approach trained on English sentiment data and cross-lingual embeddings and applied to code-mixed data. Our results show that incorporating cross-lingual embeddings increases the performance from the baseline monolingual systems. In fact, the cross-lingual embeddings are so robust that even in a transfer learning setting, the system obtains an F1-score of *0.556*, which is comparable to the supervised classification scores of *0.606* and *0.616*.

As these were first experiments to apply cross-lingual embeddings for sentiment analysis for code-mixed Hinglish data, there is still a lot of room for improvement. First, we believe the cross-lingual embeddings can still be improved, as the embeddings constructed now are generic and can be further tailored with domain information to increase performance. In addition, the cross-lingual embeddings could also be post-processed with the monolingual embeddings to make them more robust and less susceptible to degradation. Additionally, more advanced classifiers like character-based convolution networks and Transformers, can be experimented with to produce better results out of the current embeddings. Finally, both the supervised and transfer learning approaches could be combined to further improve the results by providing multiple learning sources.

To conclude, we believe transfer learning incorporating cross-lingual embeddings is a viable approach to sentiment analysis for code-mixed data. As code-mixing is a common phenomenon in multilingual societies (Parshad et al., 2016), and the issue of transliteration exist in many South-Asian languages and other languages such as Arabic, the challenges addressed in this paper also hold for many other languages and tasks. As a result, the presented approach can be used for code-mixed text processing tasks in a variety of languages, and could be an important contribution to solve the data-acquisition bottleneck for NLP for code-mixed data.

7. Bibliographical References

Artetxe, M., Labaka, G., and Agirre, E. (2018). A robust self-learning method for fully unsupervised cross-lingual mappings of word embeddings. In *Proceedings of the 56th Annual Meeting of the Association for Computational Linguistics (Volume 1: Long Papers)*, pages 789–798.

Bakliwal, A., Arora, P., and Varma, V. (2012). Hindi subjective lexicon: A lexical resource for Hindi adjective polarity classification. In *Proceedings of the Eighth International Conference on Language Resources and Evaluation (LREC'12)*, pages 1189–1196, Istanbul, Turkey. European Language Resources Association (ELRA).

Bjerva, J. and Östling, R. (2017). Cross-lingual learning of semantic textual similarity with multilingual word representations. In *Proceedings of the 21st Nordic Conference on Computational Linguistics*, pages 211–215, Gothenburg, Sweden, May. Association for Computational Linguistics.

Bojanowski, P., Grave, E., Joulin, A., and Mikolov, T. (2017). Enriching Word Vectors with Subword Information. *Transactions of the Association for Computational Linguistics*, 5:135–146.

Chen, X. and Cardie, C. (2018). Unsupervised multilingual word embeddings. In *Proceedings of the 2018 Conference on Empirical Methods in Natural Language Processing*, pages 261–270, Brussels, Belgium, October-November. Association for Computational Linguistics.

Chen, X., Sun, Y., Athiwaratkun, B., Cardie, C., and Weinberger, K. (2018). Adversarial deep averaging networks for cross-lingual sentiment classification. *Transactions of the Association for Computational Linguistics*, 6:557–570.

Conneau, A., Lample, G., Ranzato, M., Denoyer, L., and Jégou, H. (2017). Word translation without parallel data. *CoRR*, abs/1710.04087.

Conneau, A., Rinott, R., Lample, G., Williams, A., Bowman, S. R., Schwenk, H., and Stoyanov, V. (2018). Xnli: Evaluating cross-lingual sentence representations. In *Proceedings of the 2018 Conference on Empirical Methods in Natural Language Processing*, Brussels, Belgium. Association for Computational Linguistics.

Das, A. and Bandyopadhyay, S. (2010). SentiWordNet for Indian languages. In *Proceedings of the Eighth Workshop on Asian Language Resources*, pages 56–63, Beijing, China.

Das, A., Chakraborty, T., Solorio, T., Gambäck, B., Aguilar, G., Kar, S., Garrette, D., and Pykl, S. (2020). Semeval-2020 task 9: Sentimix: Sentiment analysis for code-mixed social media text. In *Proceedings of the 14th International Workshop on Semantic Evaluation (SemEval-2020)*. Association for Computational Linguistics.

Faruqui, M. and Dyer, C. (2014). Improving vector space word representations using multilingual correlation. In *Proceedings of the 14th Conference of the European Chapter of the Association for Computational Linguistics (EACL 2014)*, pages 462–471. Association for Computational Linguistics.

Gumperz, J. (1982). *Discourse Strategies*. Oxford University Press.

Hermann, K. and Blunsom, P. (2014). Multilingual models for compositional distributed semantics. In *Proceedings of the 52nd Annual Meeting of the Association for Computational Linguistics (ACL 2014)*, pages 58–68. Association for Computational Linguistics.

Joshi, A., Balamurali, A., and Bhattacharyya, P. (2010). A fall-back strategy for sentiment analysis in hindi: a case study. In *Proceedings of the 8th ICON*. Association for Computational Linguistics.

Joshi, A., Prabhu, A., Shrivastava, M., and Varma, V. (2016). Towards sub-word level compositions for sentiment analysis of Hindi-English code mixed text. In *Proceedings of COLING 2016, the 26th International Conference on Computational Linguistics*, pages 2482–2491, Osaka, Japan.

Labat, S. and Lefever, E. (2019). A classification-based approach to cognate detection combining orthographic and semantic similarity information. In G. Angelova, et al., editors, *Proceedings of Recent Advances in Natural Language Processing (RANLP 2019)*, pages 603–611, Varna, Bulgaria.

Lample, G. and Conneau, A. (2019). Cross-lingual language model pretraining. *CoRR*, abs/1901.07291.

Luong, T., Pham, H., and Manning, C. (2015). Bilingual word representations with monolingual quality in mind. In *Proceedings of the 1st Workshop on Vector Space Modeling for Natural Language Processing*, pages 151–159. Association for Computational Linguistics.

Myers-Scotton, C. (1993). *Dueling Languages: Grammatical Structure in Code-Switching*. Claredon, Oxford.

Nakov, P., Ritter, A., Rosenthal, S., Sebastiani, F., and Stoyanov, V. (2016). SemEval-2016 task 4: Sentiment analysis in twitter. In *Proceedings of the 10th International Workshop on Semantic Evaluation (SemEval-2016)*, pages 1–18, San Diego, California, June. Association for Computational Linguistics.

Nguyen, D. and Seza Dogruoz, A. (2013). Word level language identification in online multilingual communication. In *Proceedings of the 2013 Conference on Empirical Methods in Natural Language Processing (EMNLP 2013)*, pages 857–862. Association for Computational Linguistics.

Parshad, R., Bhowmick, S., Chand, V., Kumari, N., and Sinha, N. (2016). What is India speaking? Exploring the "Hinglish" invasion. *Physica A: Statistical Mechanics and its Applications*, 449:375–389.

Pratapa, A., Choudhury, M., and Sitaram, S. (2018). Word embeddings for code-mixed language processing. In *Proceedings of the 2018 Conference on Empirical Methods in Natural Language Processing (EMNLP 2018)*, pages 3067–3072. Association for Computational Linguistics.

Rijhwani, S., Sequiera, R., Choudhury, M., Bali, K., and Maddila, C. (2017). Estimating code-switching on twitter with a novel generalized word-level language detection technique. In *Proceedings of the 55th Annual Meeting of the Association for Computational Linguistics*, pages 1971–1982, Vancouver, Canada. Association for Computational Linguistics.

Sharma, A., Gupta, S., Motlani, R., Bansal, P., Shrivastava, M., Mamidi, R., and Sharma, D. (2016). Shallow parsing pipeline - hindi-english code-mixed social media text. In *Proceedings of the 2016 Conference of the North American Chapter of the Association for Computational Linguistics: Human Language Technologies*, pages 1340–1345. Association for Computational Linguistics.

Solorio, T. and Liu, Y. (2008a). Learning to predict code-switching points. In *Proceedings of the 2008 Conference on Empirical Methods in Natural Language Processing (EMNLP 2008)*, pages 973–981. Association for Computational Linguistics.

Solorio, T. and Liu, Y. (2008b). Part-of-speech tagging for english-spanish code-switched text. In *Proceedings of the 2008 Conference on Empirical Methods in Natural Language Processing (EMNLP 2008)*, pages 1051–1060. Association for Computational Linguistics.

Upadhyay, S., Faruqui, M., Dyer, C., and Roth, D. (2016). Cross-lingual models of word embeddings: An empirical comparison. In *Proceedings of the 54th Annual Meeting of the Association for Computational Linguistics (Volume 1: Long Papers)*, pages 1661–1670, Berlin, Germany, August. Association for Computational Linguistics.

Vyas, Y., Gella, S., Sharma, J., Bali, K., and Choudhury, M. (2014). Pos tagging of english-hindi code-mixed social media content. In *Proceedings of the 2014 Conference on Empirical Methods in Natural Language Processing (EMNLP 2014)*, pages 974–979. Association for Computational Linguistics.

Zhang, M., Liu, Y., Luan, H., and Sun, M. (2017). Earth mover's distance minimization for unsupervised bilingual lexicon induction. In *Proceedings of the 2017 Conference on Empirical Methods in Natural Language Processing*, pages 1934–1945, Copenhagen, Denmark, September. Association for Computational Linguistics.

Zhou, X., Wan, X., and Xiao, J. (2016). Cross-lingual sentiment classification with bilingual document representation learning. In *Proceedings of the 54th Annual Meeting of the Association for Computational Linguistics (Volume 1: Long Papers)*, pages 1403–1412, Berlin, Germany, August. Association for Computational Linguistics.

Semi-supervised Acoustic and Language Model Training for English-isiZulu Code-Switched Speech Recognition

Astik Biswas, Febe de Wet, Ewald van der Westhuizen, Thomas Niesler
Department of Electrical and Electronic Engineering, Stellenbosch University, South Africa
{abiswas, fdw, ewaldvdw, trn}@sun.ac.za

Abstract

We present an analysis of semi-supervised acoustic and language model training for English-isiZulu code-switched ASR using soap opera speech. Approximately 11 hours of untranscribed multilingual speech was transcribed automatically using four bilingual code-switching transcription systems operating in English-isiZulu, English-isiXhosa, English-Setswana and English-Sesotho. These transcriptions were incorporated into the acoustic and language model training sets. Results showed that the TDNN-F acoustic models benefit from the additional semi-supervised data and that even better performance could be achieved by including additional CNN layers. Using these CNN-TDNN-F acoustic models, a first iteration of semi-supervised training achieved an absolute mixed-language WER reduction of 3.4%, and a further 2.2% after a second iteration. Although the languages in the untranscribed data were unknown, the best results were obtained when all automatically transcribed data was used for training and not just the utterances classified as English-isiZulu. Despite reducing perplexity, the semi-supervised language model was not able to improve the ASR performance.

Keywords: code-switched speech, under-resourced languages, semi-supervised training, TDNN, CNN

1. Introduction

South Africa is a multilingual country with 11 official languages, including highly-resourced English which usually serves as a lingua-franca. The largely multilingual population commonly mix these geographically co-located languages in casual conversation. An ASR system deployed in this environment should therefore be able to process speech that includes two or more languages in one utterance.

The study and development of code-switching speech recognition systems has recently attracted increased research attention (Li and Fung, 2013; Yılmaz et al., 2018b; Adel et al., 2015; Emond et al., 2018). Language pairs that are of current research interest include English-Mandarin (Li and Fung, 2013; Vu et al., 2012; Zeng et al., 2018), Frisian-Dutch (Yılmaz et al., 2018b; Yılmaz et al., 2018a) and Hindi-English (Pandey et al., 2018). In South Africa, code-switching most often occurs between highly resourced English and one of the nine under-resourced, officially-recognised African languages.

In previous work, we showed that multilingual acoustic model training is effective for English-isiZulu code-switched ASR if additional training data from closely related languages is used (Biswas et al., 2018a). However, the 12.2 hours of training data provided by combining all our code-switching data is still too little to develop robust ASR systems.

A related study indicated that increasing the pool of in-domain training data using semi-supervised training achieved a significant improvement over the baseline acoustic model (Biswas et al., 2019). These findings motivated us to further optimise semi-supervised acoustic and language modelling training. Specifically, the effect of multiple iterations of semi-supervised training along with the application of a confidence threshold to filter the semi-supervised data was considered. We focus our investigation on one language pair, English-isiZulu, to allow for a detailed analysis of various aspects of the semi-supervised training despite the limited computational resources at our disposal.

2. Multilingual Soap Opera Corpus

The multilingual speech corpus was compiled from 626 South African soap opera episodes. Speech from these soap operas is typically spontaneous and fast, rich in code-switching and often expresses emotion, making it a challenging corpus for ASR development. The data contains examples of code-switching between South African English and four Bantu languages: isiZulu, isiXhosa, Setswana and Sesotho.

2.1. Manually Transcribed Data

Four language-balanced sets, transcribed by mother tongue speakers, were derived from the soap opera speech (van der Westhuizen and Niesler, 2018). In addition, a large but language-unbalanced (English dominated) dataset containing 21.1 hours of code-switched speech data was created (Biswas et al., 2019). The composition of this larger but unbalanced corpus is summarised in Table 2.1.. Note that all utterances in the development and test sets contain code-switching and that the balanced data is a subset of the unbalanced data.

	Language	Mono (m)	CS (m)	Subtotal (m)	Word tokens	Word types
	English	755.0	121.8	876.6	194 426	7 908
	isiZulu	92.8	57.4	150.0	24 412	6 789
Train	isiXhosa	65.1	23.8	88.8	13 825	5 630
	Sesotho	44.7	34.0	78.6	22 226	2 321
	Setswana	36.9	34.5	71.4	21 409	1 525
Dev	EZ	–	8.0	8.0	1 572	858
Test	EZ	–	30.4	30.4	5 658	3711
Total		994.4	271.5	1304.4	283 520	24 933

Table 1: Duration, in minutes (m), word type and word token counts for the unbalanced soap opera corpus. Both monolingual and code-switched (CS) durations are given.

2.2. Manually Segmented Untranscribed Data

In addition to the transcribed data introduced in the previous section, 23 290 segmented but untranscribed soap opera utterances were generated during the creation of the multi-lingual corpus. These utterances correspond to 11.1 hours of speech from 127 speakers (69 male; 57 female). The languages in the untranscribed utterances are not labelled. Several South African languages not among the five present in the transcribed data are known to occur in these segments.

3. Semi-Supervised Training

Semi-supervised techniques were used to transcribe the data introduced in Section 2.2. (Yılmaz et al., 2018b; Nallasamy et al., 2012; Thomas et al., 2013), starting with our best existing code-switching speech recognition system. In this study the manually-segmented data was transcribed twice, as illustrated in Figure 1. After each transcription pass, the acoustic models were retrained and recognition performance was evaluated in terms of WER.

We distinguish between the acoustic models used to transcribe data (`AutoT`) and those that were used to evaluate WER (`ASR`) on the test set introduced in Table 2.1.. These two models differ in the composition of their training sets. The acoustic models indicated by $AutoT_1$ in Figure 1 were trained on all the manually transcribed (ManT) data described in Section 2.1. as well as monolingual data from the NCHLT Speech Corpus (Barnard et al., 2014). These were the best available models to start semi-supervised training. The ManT and NCHLT data were subsequently pooled with the transcriptions produced by the $AutoT_1$ models to train an updated set of acoustic models ($AutoT_2$ in Figure 1) which were used to obtain a new set of transcriptions of the untranscribed data for semi-supervised training. In contrast, the acoustic models ASR_1 and ASR_2 were trained by pooling only the ManT and AutoT soap opera data; no out-of-domain NCHLT data was used.

Separate `AutoT` and `ASR` acoustic models are maintained because we use only in-domain data for semi-supervised training. This is computationally much easier, since the out-of-domain NCHLT datasets are approximately five times larger than the in-domain sets. However, it was found that better performance can be achieved in the second pass of semi-supervised training if the acoustic models maintain a similar training set composition to that used in the first pass. Hence, $AutoT_1$ and $AutoT_2$ were purpose-built, intermediate systems used solely to generate semi-supervised data.

Figure 1 also shows that each untranscribed utterance was decoded by four bilingual ASR systems. The highest confidence score was used to assign a language pair label to an utterance. In initial experiments, we added only EZ data identified in this way to the pool of multilingual training data. However, it was found that better performance could be achieved when all the AutoT data was added, and this was therefore done in the experiments reported here.

Two ways of augmenting the acoustic model training set with automatically-transcribed data were considered. First, all automatic transcriptions were pooled with the manually-labelled data. Second, utterances with a recognition confidence score below a threshold were excluded. The average confidence score across each language pair was used as a threshold. A larger variety of thresholds was not considered

for computational reasons, but this remains part of ongoing work. Confidence thresholds were applied in three ways.

1. No threshold applied in either iteration 1 or 2 of semi-supervised training. The ManT data (21.1 h) was pooled with the $AutoT_1$ data to train ASR_1 and with the $AutoT_2$ data to train ASR_2. The duration of both $AutoT_1$ and $AutoT_2$ was 11.1 h.

2. Threshold applied only in iteration 1. In this case only a subset of the $AutoT_1$ data (4.2 h) was pooled with the ManT data to train ASR_1. All 11.1 h of $AutoT_2$ data was used to train ASR_2.

3. Threshold applied in both iteration 1 and iteration 2. This resulted in a 4.2 h subset of $AutoT_1$ used to train ASR_1 and a 4.3 h subset of $AutoT_2$ used to train ASR_2.

These three scenarios are indicated by NT, T_{P1} and T_{P1P2} respectively in Table 3., which shows the number of utterances assigned to each language pair. The total number of utterances and corresponding duration of the data included in the training set is shown in the last column.

Pass		EZ	EX	ES	ET	TOTAL
1	NT	7 951	3 796	11 415	128	23 290 (11.1 h)
2		9 347	2 145	5 415	6 381	23 290 (11.1 h)
1	T_{P1}	3 704	1 731	5 338	58	10 831 (4.2 h)
2		7 888	1 756	8 798	4 869	23 290 (11.1 h)
1	T_{P1P2}	3 704	1 731	5 338	58	10 831 (4.2 h)
2		3 686	834	4 115	2 320	10 955 (4.3 h)

Table 2: Number of utterances assigned to each language pair for automatically transcribed (AutoT) data.

4. Experiments

4.1. Language Modelling

The English-isiZulu vocabulary consisted of 11 292 unique word types and was closed with respect to the training, development and test sets. The SRILM toolkit (Stolcke, 2002) was used to train a bilingual trigram language model (LM) using the transcriptions described in Section 2.1. This LM was interpolated with two monolingual trigrams trained on 471 million English and 3.2 million isiZulu words of newspaper text, respectively. The interpolation weights were chosen to minimise the development set perplexity. The resulting language model was further interpolated with LMs derived from the transcriptions produced by the process illustrated in Figure 1 to obtain a semi-supervised LM.

4.2. Acoustic Modelling

All ASR experiments were performed using the Kaldi toolkit (Povey and others, 2011) and the data described in Section 2. The automatic transcription systems were implemented using factorized time-delay neural networks (TDNN-F) (Povey et al., 2018). For multilingual training, the training sets of all four language pairs were combined. However, the acoustic models were language dependent and no phone merging across languages took place.

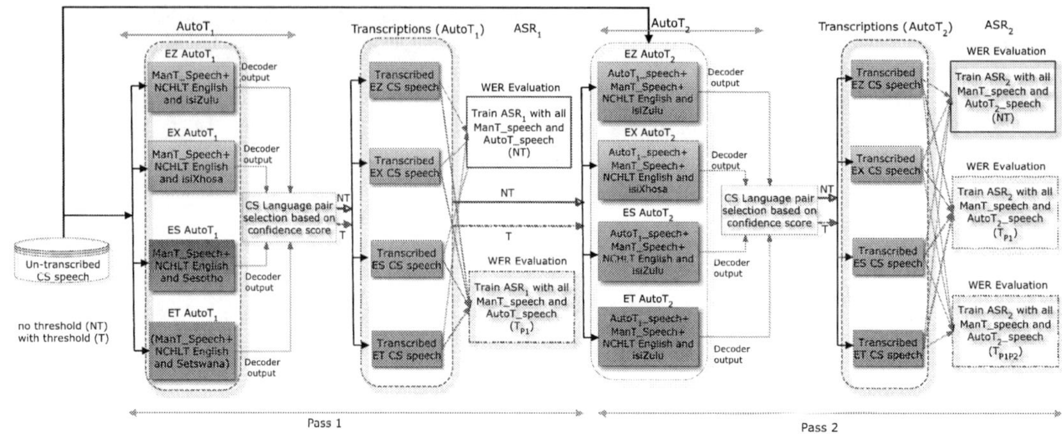

Figure 1: Semi-supervised training framework for English-isiZulu code-switched (CS) ASR.

A context-dependent GMM-HMM was trained to provide the alignments for neural network training. Three-fold data augmentation was applied prior to feature extraction (Ko et al., 2015) and the acoustic features comprised 40-dimensional MFCCs (without derivatives), 3-dimensional pitch features and 100-dimensional i-vectors for speaker adaptation.

We used two types of neural network-based acoustic model architectures: (1) TDNN-F with 10 time-delay layers followed by a rank reduction layer trained using the Kaldi Librispeech recipe (version 5.2.164) and (2) CNN-TDNN-F consisting of two CNN layers followed by the TDNN-F architecture. TDNN-F models have been shown to be effective in under-resourced scenarios (Povey et al., 2018). The locality, weight sharing and pooling properties of the CNNs have been shown to benefit ASR (Abdel-Hamid et al., 2014). The default recipe parameters were used during neural network training. In a final training step the multilingual acoustic models were adapted with English-isiZulu code-switched speech.

5. Results and Discussion

5.1. Language Modelling

Table 5.1. shows the test set perplexities (PP) for the LM configurations described in Section 4.1. The baseline language model, LM_0, was trained on the English-isiZulu acoustic training data transcriptions as well as monolingual English and isiZulu text (Biswas et al., 2018b). LM_0 was also interpolated with trigram LMs trained on the 1-best and 10-best outputs of $AutoT_2$ respectively. MPP indicates monolingual perplexity and is calculated over monolingual stretches of text only, omitting points at which the language alternates. CPP indicates code-switch perplexity and is calculated only over language switch points. Therefore CPP indicates the uncertainty of the first word following a language switch.

Table 5.1. shows that, relative to the baseline, adding automatically generated English-isiZulu transcriptions to the language model training data improves the overall perplexity for both the development and test sets. The per-language results show that this improvement is due to a lower isiZulu

LM	PP (dev)	PP	MPP_E	MPP_Z	MPP	CPP
LM_0 (baseline)	425.8	601.7	121.2	777.8	358.1	3 292.0
LM_0 + 1-best	416.1	587.4	123.1	743.6	351.1	3 160.3
LM_0 + 10-best	408.2	583.6	124.4	722.8	346.9	3 205.2

Table 3: Perplexity of bilingual English-isiZulu trigram LMs.

perplexity, while English suffers a small deterioration. CPP is reduced when incorporating the 1-best automatic transcriptions but less so when incorporating the 10-best. This indicates that the code-switches present in the 1-best outputs are more representative of the unseen test set switches than those present in the 10-best output.

5.2. Acoustic Modelling

ASR performance was evaluated on the English-isiZulu test set for various configurations of the ASR_1 and ASR_2 systems.

5.2.1. ASR_1

Table 5.2.1. reports WER results for different configurations of ASR_1. Previously-reported results using a balanced subset of the corpus described in Section 2.1. are reproduced in rows 1 and 2. Language specific WERs are provided for the test set but not the development set.

The results in row 4 of the table show that, when the TDNN-F network is preceded by two CNN layers, test set recognition performance improves by 1.9% absolute. Row 5, on the other hand, shows that the inclusion of the automatically-transcribed English-isiZulu utterances reduces the test set WER of the TDNN-F models by 1.8% absolute. This improvement increases by an additional 0.8% absolute when including all the automatically transcribed data and not just the English-isiZulu utterances, as shown in row 6. Row 7 shows that the performance of the CNN-TDNN-F system is also enhanced by including the automatically transcribed data. In all the above cases, the WER improvements are seen not only overall but also in the English and isiZulu language-specific error rates.

Finally, the results in row 8 illustrate the impact of applying a confidence threshold to decide which automatically-transcribed utterances to include in the training set. The values in the table indicate that the mixed WER deteriorates marginally and that the English WER improves at the cost of a higher isiZulu WER.

	System configuration	Dev	Test	WER_E	WER_Z
1	ManT (balanced) TDNN-LSTM (Biswas et al., 2018a)	47.4	55.8	50.0	60.1
2	ManT (balanced) TDNN-BLSTM (Biswas et al., 2018b)	47.1	53.1	47.6	57.2
3	ManT (baseline) TDNN-F	41.3	47.4	41.8	51.8
4	ManT CNN-TDNN-F	40.8	45.6	40.0	49.9
5	ManT + AutoT$_1$ (EZ,NT) TDNN-F	41.2	45.7	39.6	50.3
6	ManT + AutoT$_1$ (All,NT) TDNN-F	39.5	44.9	38.9	49.6
7	ManT + AutoT$_1$ (All,NT) CNN-TDNN-F (Biswas et al., 2019)	**38.2**	**44.0**	37.9	48.7
8	ManT + AutoT$_1$ (All,T_{P1}) CNN-TDNN-F	38.8	44.2	36.6	50.1

Table 4: WER (%) on the English-isiZulu development (dev) and test sets for different configurations of ASR_1.

5.2.2. ASR$_2$

The results for the second iteration of semi-supervised training are reported in Table 5.2.2.. In all cases the ManT data was pooled with all the AutoT data and not just the EZ sub-set as was done in row 5 of Table 5.2.1.. Only the results using the CNN-TDNN-F acoustic models are shown, since this gave consistently superior performance in Table 5.2.1..

	Training data	LM	Dev	Test	WER_E	WER_Z
1	ManT + AutoT$_2$ (NT)	LM$_0$	38.6	42.5	36.2	47.6
2	ManT + AutoT$_2$ (T_{P1})	LM$_0$	38.0	43.1	37.5	47.4
3	ManT + AutoT$_2$ (T_{P1P2})	LM$_0$	40.1	43.9	34.2	51.3
4	ManT + AutoT$_2$ (NT, tuned)	LM$_0$	36.5	41.9	33.0	48.8
5		LM$_0$ + 1-best	**36.5**	**41.8**	33.9	47.9
6		LM$_0$ + 10-best	36.7	42.0	34.0	48.1

Table 5: WER (%) on the English-isiZulu development (dev) and test sets for different configurations of ASR_2.

A comparison between row 1 in Table 5.2.2. and row 7 in Table 5.2.1. reveals that a second pass of retraining affords a further 1.5% absolute reduction in test set WER. This was found to be statistically significant at more than 95% confidence level using bootstrap interval estimation (Bisani and Ney, 2004). Retraining ASR$_2$ with a threshold applied only to the output of AutoT$_1$ results in a slightly higher WER on the test set (row 2). Applying thresholds in both passes (row 3) improved the English WER but resulted in a substantial deterioration in isiZulu WER. This result suggests that, for the threshold value used here, English benefits from the exclusion of low-confidence automatically transcribed data while isiZulu does not. Thus, further study on the optimum threshold configuration is required.

The results in row 4 of Table 5.2.2. show that a further 0.6% absolute WER reduction can be achieved for the test set by tuning the learning rate during adaptation. Rows 5 and 6 show that retraining the LM on text that includes automatic transcriptions hardly influences recognition performance. Thus, although semi-supervised training led to appreciable improvements in the acoustic models, the corresponding positive effects on the language model were marginal.

A detailed analysis of different ASR outputs is shown in Table 5.2.2.. The analysis confirms that semi-supervised training resulted in substantial improvements in the English and isiZulu word correct accuracy. The results also reveal a substantial improvement in bigram correct accuracy at the 1 464 code-switch points occurring in the test set, where bigram correct accuracy (%) is defined as the percentage of words correctly recognised immediately after code-switch points.

Accuracy (%)	Table 4 (Row 3)	Table 4 (Row 4)	Table 4 (Row 7)	Table 4 (Row 8)	Table 5 (Row 4)
Eng token correct	59.8	61.5	64.5	65.4	68.8
Zul token correct	50.1	51.4	53.2	51.6	53.5
Word correct after switch	53.4	55.6	58.3	57.6	60.9
Zul word correct after switch	49.7	51.4	53.6	51.6	54.4
English word correct after switch	56.7	59.3	62.5	62.9	66.7
Language correct after switch	76.8	76.9	79.1	79.0	81.6
Code-switch bigram correct	29.0	30.8	33.3	32.2	35.6

Table 6: Detailed analysis of ASR accuracy for different acoustic models.

6. Conclusion

We have applied semi-supervised training to improve ASR for under-resourced code-switched English-isiZulu speech. Four different automatic transcription systems were used in two phases to decode 11 hours of multilingual, manually segmented but untranscribed soap opera speech. We found that by including CNN layers, CNN-TDNN-F acoustic models outperformed TDNN-F models on the code-switched speech. Furthermore, semi-supervised training provided a further absolute reduction of 5.5% in WER for the CNN-TDNN-F system. While the automatically transcribed English-isiZulu text data reduced language model perplexity, this improvement did not lead to a reduction in WER. By selective data inclusion using a confidence threshold, approximately 60% of the automatically transcribed data could be discarded at minimal loss in recognition performance. A more thorough investigation of this threshold remains part of ongoing work. We also aim to further extend the pool of training data by incorporating speaker and language diarisation systems to allow automatic segmentation of new audio.

7. Acknowledgements

We would like to thank the Department of Arts & Culture (DAC) of the South African government for funding this research. We are grateful to e.tv and Yula Quinn at Rhythm City, as well as the SABC and Human Stark at Generations: The Legacy, for assistance with data compilation. We also gratefully acknowledge the support of the NVIDIA corporation for the donation of GPU equipment.

8. Bibliographical References

Abdel-Hamid, O., Mohamed, A.-R., Jiang, H., Deng, L., Penn, G., and Yu, D. (2014). Convolutional neural networks for speech recognition. *IEEE/ACM Transactions on Audio, Speech, and Language Processing*, 22(10):1533–1545.

Adel, H., Vu, N. T., Kirchhoff, K., Telaar, D., and Schultz, T. (2015). Syntactic and semantic features for code-switching factored language models. *IEEE Transactions on Audio, Speech, and Language Processing*, 23(3):431–440.

Barnard, E., Davel, M. H., Heerden, C. v., de Wet, F., and Badenhorst, J. (2014). The NCHLT speech corpus of the South African languages. In *Proc. SLTU*, St Petersburg, Russia.

Bisani, M. and Ney, H. (2004). Bootstrap estimates for confidence intervals in ASR performance evaluation. In *Proc. ICASSP*, Montreal, Canada.

Biswas, A., de Wet, F., van der Westhuizen, E., Yılmaz, E., and Niesler, T. R. (2018a). Multilingual neural network acoustic modelling for ASR of under-resourced English-isiZulu code-switched speech. In *Proc. Interspeech*, Hyderabad, India.

Biswas, A., van der Westhuizen, E., Niesler, T. R., and de Wet, F. (2018b). Improving ASR for code-switched speech in under-resourced languages using out-of-domain data. In *Proc. SLTU*, Gurugram, India.

Biswas, A., Yılmaz, E., de Wet, F., van der Westhuizen, E., and Niesler, T. R. (2019). Semi-supervised acoustic model training for five-lingual code-switched ASR. In *Proc. Interspeech*, Graz, Austria.

Emond, J., Ramabhadran, B., Roark, B., Moreno, P., and Ma, M. (2018). Transliteration based approaches to improve code-switched speech recognition performance. In *Proc. SLT*, Athens, Greece.

Ko, T., Peddinti, V., Povey, D., and Khudanpur, S. (2015). Audio augmentation for speech recognition. In *Proc. Interspeech*, Dresdan, Germany.

Li, Y. and Fung, P. (2013). Improved mixed language speech recognition using asymmetric acoustic model and language model with code-switch inversion constraints. In *Proc. ICASSP*, Vancouver, Canada.

Nallasamy, U., Metze, F., and Schultz, T. (2012). Semi-supervised learning for speech recognition in the context of accent adaptation. In *Symposium on Machine Learning in Speech and Language Processing*, Portland, Oregon, USA.

Pandey, A., Srivastava, B. M. L., Kumar, R., Nellore, B. T., Teja, K. S., and Gangashetty, S. V. (2018). Phonetically balanced code-mixed speech corpus for Hindi-English automatic speech recognition. In *Proc. LREC*, Miyazaki, Japan.

Povey, D. et al. (2011). The Kaldi speech recognition toolkit. In *Proc. ASRU*, Hawaii, USA.

Povey, D., Cheng, G., Wang, Y., Li, K., Xu, H., Yarmohammadi, M., and Khudanpur, S. (2018). Semi-orthogonal low-rank matrix factorization for deep neural networks. In *Proc. Interspeech*, Graz, Austria.

Stolcke, A. (2002). SRILM – An extensible language modeling toolkit. In *Proc. ICSLP*, Denver, USA.

Thomas, S., Seltzer, M. L., Church, K., and Hermansky, H. (2013). Deep neural network features and semi-supervised training for low resource speech recognition. In *Proc. ICASSP*, Vancouver, Canada.

van der Westhuizen, E. and Niesler, T. R. (2018). A first South African corpus of multilingual code-switched soap opera speech. In *Proc. LREC*, Miyazaki, Japan.

Vu, N. T., Lyu, D.-C., Weiner, J., Telaar, D., Schlippe, T., Blaicher, F., Chng, E.-S., Schultz, T., and Li, H. (2012). A first speech recognition system for Mandarin-English code-switch conversational speech. In *Proc. ICASSP*, Kyoto, Japan.

Yılmaz, E., Biswas, A., van der Westhuizen, E., de Wet, F., and Niesler, T. R. (2018a). Building a unified code-switching ASR system for South African languages. In *Proc. Interspeech*, Hyderabad, India.

Yılmaz, E., McLaren, M., van den Heuvel, H., and van Leeuwen, D. A. (2018b). Semi-supervised acoustic model training for speech with code-switching. *Speech Communication*, 105:12–22.

Zeng, Z., Khassanov, Y., Pham, V. T., Xu, H., Chng, E. S., and Li, H. (2018). On the end-to-end solution to Mandarin-English code-switching speech recognition. *arXiv preprint arXiv:1811.00241*.

Proceedings of the LREC 2020 – 4th Workshop on Computational Approaches to Code Switching, pages 57–64
Language Resources and Evaluation Conference (LREC 2020), Marseille, 11–16 May 2020
European Language Resources Association (ELRA), licensed under CC-BY-NC

Code-Mixed Parse Trees and How to Find Them

Anirudh Srinivasan[1] , Sandipan Dandapat[2], Monojit Choudhury[1]
[1]Microsoft Research, India [2]Microsoft R&D, India
{t-ansrin, sadandap, monojitc}@microsoft.com

Abstract

In this paper, we explore the methods of obtaining parse trees of code-mixed sentences and analyse the obtained trees. Existing work has shown that linguistic theories can be used to generate code-mixed sentences from a set of parallel sentences. We build upon this work, using one of these theories, the Equivalence-Constraint theory to obtain the parse trees of synthetically generated code-mixed sentences and evaluate them with a neural constituency parser. We highlight the lack of a dataset non-synthetic code-mixed constituency parse trees and how it makes our evaluation difficult. To complete our evaluation, we convert a code-mixed dependency parse tree set into "pseudo constituency trees" and find that a parser trained on synthetically generated trees is able to decently parse these as well.

Keywords: Parse Trees, Constituency Parsing, Code-mixing

1. Introduction

Code-mixing is a phenomenon observed in multilingual societies all throughout the world. Although it started off as mainly a spoken phenomenon, the need for computational methods for processing code-mixed text is ever growing as people are now code-mixing on social media and other online platforms more and more (Rijhwani et al., 2017).

Most work focusing on computational methods for code-mixing have been on tasks like LID (Solorio et al., 2014; Sequiera et al., 2015), NER (Aguilar et al., 2018) and POS tagging (Vyas et al., 2014). Although there are some works on code-mixed dependency parsing (Partanen et al., 2018; Bhat et al., 2018), there is no work that has focused on obtaining parse trees and the task of constituency parsing.

Having parse trees and a constituency parser for any language is extremely useful. It can be used for understanding the syntax of a sentence and checking whether a sentence is grammatically valid or not. Parse trees can also be used to build a probabilistic context free grammar (PCFG) that would help us understand the usage of different grammatical elements.

The work in this paper makes 3 contributions to the area of code-mixed parsing. Firstly, we propose a technique that modifies existing linguistic theory based code-mixed sentence generation processes to obtain parse trees of the sentences. The trees produced are also annotated in a manner that captures the parallels between the mixed languages that are used during the generation process. Secondly, we use these synthetic trees to train a neural constituency parser and evaluate the parser on synthetic and non-synthetic trees. This evaluation was not straightforward as there doesn't exist a set of non-synthetic code-mixed constituency trees. To address this issue, as the third contribution of the paper, we convert code-mixed dependency trees into what we call as "pseudo constituency trees" and show that the parser is able to parse these as well.

The rest of the paper is organized as follows. Section 2 talks about linguistic theories for code-mixing and how they can be used to obtain code-mixed parse trees. Section 3 talks about neural constituency parsers and the parsing technique chosen for our testing. Section 4 describes the evaluation method for the parser and results on synthetic data. Section 5 talks about further evaluating the parser using non-synthetic data and Section 6 concludes our discussion.

2. Obtaining Code-Mixed Parse Trees

2.1. Background

Researchers in linguistics have proposed multiple theories that aim to model code-mixing from a linguistics perspective. (Poplack, 1980; Sankoff, 1998; Joshi, 1982; Milroy, 1995; Di Sciullo et al., 1986; Belazi et al., 1994). On the whole, these theories draw parallels between the parse trees of a pair of parallel sentences in 2 languages and model code-mixing as the substitution of a subtree in one language with its equivalent in the other language, assuming that a set of conditions are satisfied. One of these theories is the Equivalence Constraint (EC) theory (Poplack, 1980; Sankoff, 1998). The work of Bhat et al. (2016) and Pratapa et al. (2018) make use of the EC theory to generate synthetic code-mixed sentences given a pair of parallel sentences. They show that using these generated sentences in language modeling showed an improvement in perplexity on a test set of non-synthetic sentences.

2.2. Generating Synthetic Code-Mixed Sentences

The method for generating code-mixed sentences in Bhat et al. (2016) first obtains equivalent parse trees of the parallel sentences in their respective languages. The method is briefly described here. The paper can be referred to for a detailed explanation. Assuming that $L1$ and $L2$ are the 2 languages,

1. Obtain a sentence in $L1$, its equivalent in $L2$ and a word level alignment between the two sentences

2. Obtain the parse tree of either of the sentences. If $L1$, is English, this can be done using a tool like the Stanford Parser (Klein and Manning, 2003)

3. Once the $L1$ tree is obtained, use the word level alignments to project the $L2$ words onto the $L1$ tree in a bottom-up manner. In this manner, the $L2$ tree is obtained

Figure 1a and 1b show monolingual trees for $L1$ and $L2$. Having these equivalent trees, EC theory allows the substitution of any number of words in the $L1$ tree with their equivalents in $L2$ tree as long as set of constraints are satisfied.

Author can be contacted at anirudhsriniv@gmail.com

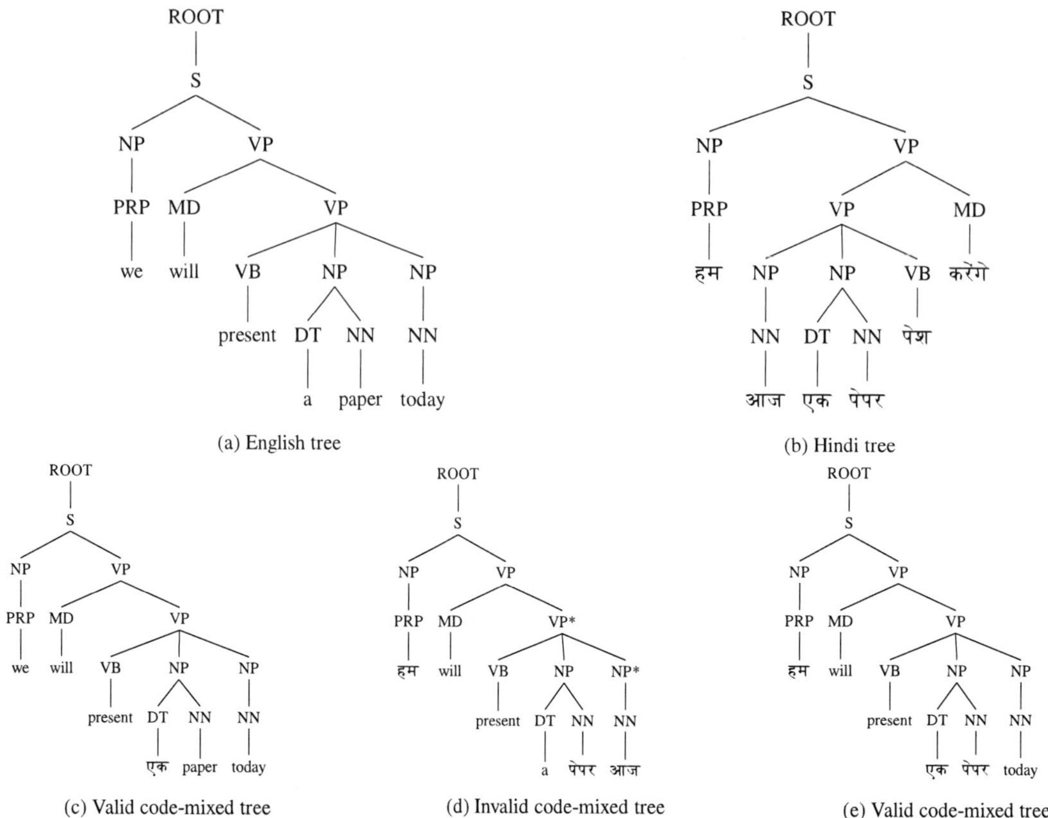

Figure 1: Monolingual and intermediate code-mixed trees. $L1$ is English and $L2$ is Hindi. Figure 1d is an invalid tree. The production being applied at the VP marked with * is the English production, which means that only the English productions can be applied for the terms on its RHS. However, the NP node on its RHS (marked with *) is deriving a Hindi word, which it is not allowed to, resulting in the tree being invalid. Had the English word been there (today, instead of आज), it would have been a valid sentence. Figures 1c and 1e are valid trees.

These constraints are detailed in the aforementioned paper. We will elaborate on one of these constraints in the next section. Since we are working at the parse tree level, we directly obtain the parse tree of the generated sentence every time we make substitutions. Figures 1c, 1d and 1e depict intermediate code-mixed trees obtained by making substitutions. The tree in Figure 1d is invalid and we explain why at the end of the next section.

2.3. EC Theory: Word Order

We focus on one of the EC theory constraints, as this will help us in better annotating the parse trees we obtain. For every production $u_0 \rightarrow u_1 u_2 ... u_n$ in the $L1$ tree, there must exist an equivalent production $v_0 \rightarrow v_1 v_2 ... v_n$ in the $L2$ tree such that

- u_0 and v_0 are the same non-terminal

- There exists a unique one-one mapping from the non-terminals in $u_1, u_2, ... u_n$ to the non-terminals in $v_1, v_2, ... v_n$

This simplifies down to 2 conditions: the LHS of the both the productions are the same and the RHS of both the pro-

ductions have the same set of terms, possibly in a different order.

Given these definitions, we describe one of the constraints that are verified on the intermediate code-mixed tree (obtained after substitution of words from one language to the other). Starting in a bottom up manner, each non-terminal is assigned 2 language tags, one based on the word order of the production it's derived from and one based on the word order of the production being applied at it. If these tags match, this check continues up the tree. If the tags don't match at any point, the sentence is considered to be invalid.

This simplifies down to each production in the tree having a word order in its RHS that is either the $L1$ order or the $L2$ order, and that order determining which production ($L1$ or $L2$) can be applied for each term on the RHS. If the word order is same for both $L1$ and $L2$, either language's production can be applied for the terms on the RHS. Figure 1d shows an invalid code-mixed tree. The NP marked with * is assigned the tag of h from below as it is deriving a Hindi word and the tag e from above as the English word order is being applied at its parent node VP (marked with *), leading to a mismatch and making the sentence invalid.

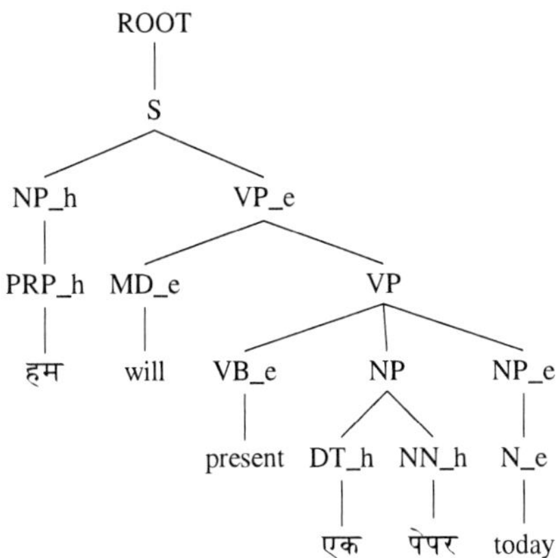

Figure 2: The final annotated code-mixed parse tree for tree in Figure 1e.

2.4. Annotating CM Parse Trees

We obtain the code-mixed trees directly each time we make substitutions in the monolingual trees. However, these simple trees do not capture the information provided by EC theory used in generating the tree. To address this, we annotate each non-terminal in the tree with a tag. This tag is determined by the language whose production (word order) was applied at that non-terminal. For leaf nodes, this would be the language of the word that takes it's place. For intermediate nodes, we added '_e' or '_h' depending on whether the $L1$ or $L2$ production was applied. This will ensure that the parser trained on these trees will learn the differences in word order for the productions in different languages. In cases where the word order is same for both languages, we do not add a tag. This is so that a parser will learn that the word order for that production would be same in both languages. Figure 2 shows the final tree generated by the process for the tree in Figure 1e.

3. Constituency Parsing

3.1. Background

Constituency parsing is the task of generating a valid parse tree given a sentence as input. One of the simplest methods for this task is the CKY algorithm (Younger, 1967). This algorithm takes in a set of CFG productions and builds up a tree for a sentence using a dynamic programming algorithm. There are variations of this algorithm that work with a Probabilistic CFG as well (Booth and Thompson, 1973).

Most of the early neural network parsers were simple encoder-decoder approaches where the sentence would be taken in by the encoder and the decoder would have to output the tree with no extra information being provided about a tree structure (Vinyals et al., 2015). These later evolved into methods where the decoder was constrained to output tokens that conformed to a valid tree structure (Ballesteros et al., 2015; Dyer et al., 2016). One negative aspect of these early neural methods is that they required extensive feature engineering to perform well (Thang et al., 2015).

3.2. Span Based Constituency Parsing

Span based parsing methods use a function to assign scores to spans in the sentence and use the CKY algorithm to build up

Dataset	Size	Height	RHS Length
En-Hi Train	421710	7.05 (1.96)	2.22 (2.34)
En-Hi Synth. Test	2740	7.10 (2.02)	2.21 (2.28)
En-Hi Real. Test	1381	5.40 (1.06)	3.38 (1.60)
En-Es Train	421710	8.16 (2.31)	1.75 (1.16)
En-Es Synth. Test	2542	8.13 (2.24)	1.73 (1.12)

Table 1: Statistics about Train and Test Datasets. Mean and Standard deviation (in brackets) reported for tree height and length of right hand size of productions.

the tree given these scores. Finkel et al. (2008) use Conditional Random Fields (CRFs) for the scoring purpose. More recently, there has been a line of work where neural networks have been used to score the spans, starting off with Durrett and Klein (2015) where a fixed-window based method is used. Stern et al. (2017) build upon this work by using RNNs instead of a fixed-window for the scoring and Kitaev and Klein (2018) use a transformer instead of the RNN. These methods achieve performance that is superior to the early neural network parsers without the complex feature engineering associated with most of them.

3.3. Choice of Parser

We chose the span-based parser of Kitaev and Klein (2018)[1] for evaluating our trees. We chose this method as it requires only a set of trees as input for training and no information about the grammar of the language(s). This method achieves near state of the art performance on the Penn Treebank WSJ set.

This model runs the embedding of each token in the sentence through a transformer layer to produce contextual embeddings for each token, which are used to compute embeddings for each span in the sentence. This is then run through a scoring layer to produce scores for each span. These scores are used in a modified CKY-style parser to build up the most probable tree. For computing initial embedding of each token, we experiment with word embeddings over the combined vocabulary space of both languages and with multilingual BERT[2] (Devlin et al., 2019) (mBERT), which produces subword level embeddings. Lastly, the parsing model also learns to predict POS tags of tokens (using it while parsing), so we also report the POS tagging accuracy.

4. Evaluation

We created train, dev and test sets of synthetic trees from independent sets of parallel sentences, so there is no overlap in the trees between the 3 sets. Table 1 contains some statistics about the datasets. For both language pairs, we obtained parallel corpora by taking English sentences and running them through Bing Translator to obtain the parallel sentences. This allows us to perform this technique for languages that do not have large parallel corpora available for them. Since we are using an MT system, we end up with parallel sentences that are less likely to be semantic equivalents of each other and

---

[1] `https://github.com/nikitakit/self-attentive-parser`

[2] `https://github.com/google-research/bert/blob/master/multilingual.md`

	Hindi-English		Spanish-English	
Model	**Synth. Test**		**Synth. Test**	
	F1	POS	F1	POS
Word	38.22	96.07	33.20	90.23
mBERT	40.70	99.18	40.32	96.41

Table 2: Parsing F1 scores and POS tagging accuracies on Hindi-English and Spanish-English.

more likely to have one-one mapping between the words of both languages.

For Hindi-English, we used the sentences from the IITB Hi-En corpus (Kunchukuttan et al., 2018) which consists of sentences from multiple domains. For Spanish-English, we used the sentences from the corpus by Rijhwani et al. (2017) that mainly consists of sentences from social media (Twitter). We report parsing F1 scores for both these languages along with POS tagging accuracies. We call these test sets as "Synth. Test" as they contain synthetically generated trees. We report these results in Table 2.

4.1. Results

For Hindi-English we find that on our synthetic test set, we are able to get a F1 score of 38.22 using word embeddings. Using mBERT, we are able to get an increase of 2 points in the score. Both models are able to achieve high accuracies on POS tagging. For Spanish-English, similar to Hindi-English, using mBERT causes a boost in the F1 measure for parsing. For reference, we report results for English from (Kitaev and Klein, 2018) (which happens to be near state of the art), in which they obtain an F1 score of 92.67 using this same parsing technique.

4.2. Monolingual - Code-Mixed Performance Gap Analysis

Given that there is a big gap in the performance of our code-mixed parser and a state of the art (SOTA) parser on English, we perform a series of experiments with the aim of finding out the following: How much does each of the steps of our generation method contribute to the drop in the parser's performance? The processing done by our method can be divided into 3 stages:

1. Parsing the English sentence using the Stanford parser

2. Using alignments to project the English tree to obtain the $L2$ tree and an equivalent English tree

3. Substituting between the two trees to obtain a code-mixed tree

We already have the parsing results for trees produced after Step 3. We obtain trees produced after Step 1 and 2, train the parser on these trees and report the results on a test set. These trees are monolingual as code-mixing is done only in Step 3. We report results on the English trees that were used for Spanish-English code-mixing. These results are in Table 3.

We observe that there is a 20% drop in F1 comparing Step 1 to the SOTA English performance. This drop is due to

Parsing English Sentence

Model	**F1**
Word	67.98
mBERT	69.31

Obtaining equivalent English and $L2$ trees using alignements

Model	**F1**
Word	47.55
mBERT	50.93

Code-Mixing

Model	**F1**
Word	33.20
mBERT	40.32

Table 3: Parsing F1 scores and POS tagging accuracies after every step of our method. The first 2 tables are on monolingual (English) trees, while the third one is on code-mixed (Spanish-English) trees.

the errors introduced by using the Stanford parser to parse the English sentences. When we move from Step 1 to Step 2, we observe another 20% drop. This is the result of our method of projecting the English tree using alignments to obtain the $L2$ tree. The drop from Step 2 to Step 3 is around 10%. This is the actual complexity introduced to the parser by code-mixing, a much smaller difference than the 50% estimate from before.

We can draw the following conclusions from this analysis. The complexity introduced by code-mixing brings in only a 10% drop in performance of the parser. The major reasons for the drop are the steps that obtain the parse trees for English and $L2$. Improvements to this technique can help in obtaining much better code-mixed parse trees.

5. Further Evaluation

5.1. Better Evaluation Methods: Using Non-Synthetic Trees

Evaluating the parser on synthetically generated trees alone is not sufficient. To get a thorough estimate of the usefulness of our synthetically generated trees, we have to take a parser trained on these trees and evaluate it on non-synthetic (real) trees. To accomplish, one would need a dataset of constituency parse trees of code-mixed sentences and to the best of our knowledge, such a dataset does not exist.

To address this and perform a more complete evaluation of our trees, we use of the work by Bhat et al. (2018) to come up with an evaluation technique. Their work proposes a Hindi-English code-mixed dependency parsing dataset. Dependency parse trees have a structure that is very different to constituency parse trees (see Figure 3). We convert these dependency trees to pseudo constituency trees and evaluate the parser with them.

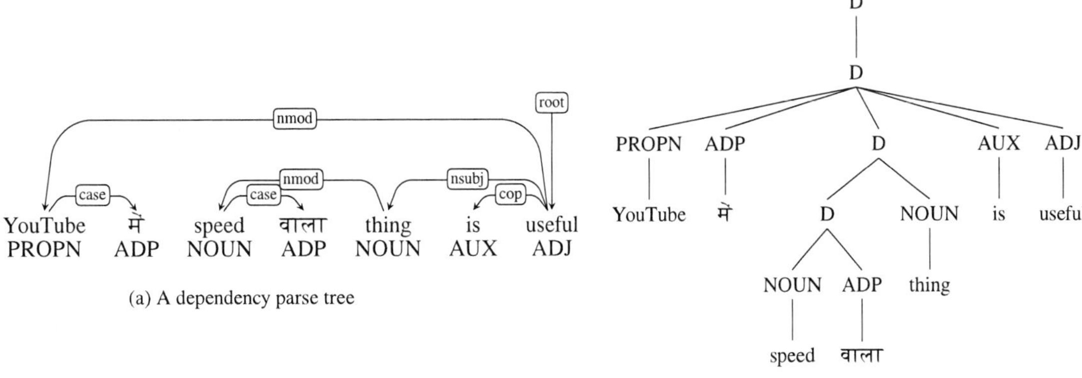

(a) A dependency parse tree

(b) The converted constituency parse tree

Figure 3: A dependency parse tree and the constituency tree obtained by the conversion technique used.

5.2. Converting Dependency Trees to Constituency Trees

Although there has been a lot of recent work on converting dependency trees to constituency trees (Xia et al., 2008; Wang and Zong, 2010; Lee and Wang, 2016), most of these works require having the golden constituency tree for a dependency tree and train a machine learning based algorithm on such a golden tree set to learn the conversion. Since these resources are something not available for our case, we focus on the works of Collins et al. (1999) and Xia and Palmer (2001). These propose an algorithm that will convert a dependency tree to a constituency tree in a deterministic fashion, outputting the structure alone of the constituency tree. This algorithm does not assign labels to intermediate nodes in the tree, a step that the aforementioned machine learning based algorithms try to achieve using labelled data.

5.3. Evaluation Methodology

We make use of Algorithm 2 from Xia and Palmer (2001) to convert the dependency trees in the train set of Bhat et al. (2018) (1381 tweets) to constituency trees. One aspect to note is that while this dataset is from Twitter, our synthetic trees are from a multiple-domain dataset. We assign the nonterminals without labels (all non-terminal except leaf level ones) the label 'D' and refer to the produced trees as pseudo constituency trees. Figure 3 shows a dependency parse tree and the pseudo constituency tree obtained by converting it. We use this as a test set on our trained parsers along with a metric we call "Unlabelled F1". This metric is needed as we don't have the labels for intermediate non-terminals, resulting in skewed scores being produced if we used the F1 score as per its original definition.

As per its original definition, the F1 score for parsing is calculated using precision and recall computed over successes and failures in the following manner: success is when a particular span in the sentence contains the same parent in the gold and the generated trees with the parent labels being the same, failure being otherwise. For our Unlabelled F1 measure, we relax the criterion of checking if the parent's labels match. We report this F1 score and POS accuracies in Table 4 under the Real Test column. We also calculate the Unla-

Model	Real Test		Synth. Test	
	F1*	POS	F1*	POS
Word	30.32	40.25	46.93	96.07
mBERT	30.60	41.31	49.98	99.18

Table 4: *Unlabelled F1 and POS accuracies on the Hindi-English set of converted dependency trees.

belled F1 score for our Synth. Test set and report it and the POS accuracies(same value as in 2) for reference. Since we do not have English-Spanish dependency trees, we do not report any results on a Real Test set for that language pair.

5.4. Results & Error Analysis

We observe that the neural parser is able to perform decently on the Real Test set. There is a performance gap between the performance on this and on the synthetic test set. We also note that there is a huge gap in the POS tagging accuracy between the 2 sets. The domain mismatch between Real. Test and Synth. Test could contribute to the performance difference. We elaborate below on another possible reason.

Observing the distributions of tree height and production RHS length in Table 1, we observe a difference between the Train/Synth Test and Real Test sets. Given that these values (height, production RHS length) are integers and not continuous values, a difference of even 1 for their mean values is significant. We theorize that this is the side-effect of the algorithm used to convert dependency trees to constituency trees. In their work, Xia and Palmer (2001) refer to Algorithm 2, the algorithm that we've used, as the "Flattest Possible" algorithm, producing trees that are flatter (less in height) and wider (longer RHS of productions). This is clearly visible in our case, as the mean height is lesser and mean RHS length is more when comparing Real Test to both Train and Synth Test. Given this difference in the distribution between the train and test, the parser is not able to perform as well.

5.4.1. Error Analysis

We performed an analysis of where the parser makes errors and have listed some observations below. Appendix A contains the gold tree from Real Test and the parser's predictions with more detailed explanations on how the parser is failing.

1. POS tag errors cause the parser to not capture smaller subtrees well

2. Longer sentences result in the parser not being able to capture any tree structure at all (i.e the root node derives most of the leaf nodes directly)

6. Conclusion

We present a technique to generate code-mixed parse trees given a pair of parallel sentences. We train a neural parser on these trees and report parsing F1 scores on a test set of generated trees. We also look into obtaining an evaluation set of non-synthetic trees and highlight the lack of such a resource in the community. Using an existing dependency parse resource, we evaluate our parser and observe that it is able to parse non-synthetic sentences as well, albeit not as well as it is able to perform on a set of synthetic sentences. The lack of code-mixed constituency parse set is something we've had to work around and the computational linguistics community would really benefit if such a resource exists.

A neural parser capable of performing on code-mixed sentences is a useful tool to have. Such a parser could be used to analyze code-mixed corpora and obtain statistics much more useful than values like Code-Mixing Index (CMI), Switching Point Fraction(SPF) etc.., statistics like what grammatical elements are likely to be switched more frequently and what are likely to be not. This information could further be used to sample from a set of large generated sentences to obtain more realistic sentences.

7. Bibliographical References

Aguilar, G., AlGhamdi, F., Soto, V., Diab, M., Hirschberg, J., and Solorio, T. (2018). Named entity recognition on code-switched data: Overview of the CALCS 2018 shared task. In *Proceedings of the Third Workshop on Computational Approaches to Linguistic Code-Switching*, pages 138–147, Melbourne, Australia, July. Association for Computational Linguistics.

Ballesteros, M., Dyer, C., and Smith, N. A. (2015). Improved transition-based parsing by modeling characters instead of words with lstms.

Belazi, H. M., Rubin, E. J., and Toribio, A. J. (1994). Code switching and x-bar theory: The functional head constraint. *Linguistic inquiry*, pages 221–237.

Bhat, G., Choudhury, M., and Bali, K. (2016). Grammatical constraints on intra-sentential code-switching: From theories to working models.

Bhat, I., Bhat, R. A., Shrivastava, M., and Sharma, D. (2018). Universal dependency parsing for hindi-english code-switching. In *Proceedings of the 2018 Conference of the North American Chapter of the Association for Computational Linguistics: Human Language Technologies, Volume 1 (Long Papers)*, volume 1, pages 987–998.

Booth, T. L. and Thompson, R. A. (1973). Applying probability measures to abstract languages. *IEEE transactions on Computers*, 100(5):442–450.

Collins, M., Hajic, J., Ramshaw, L., and Tillmann, C. (1999). A statistical parser for Czech. In *Proceedings of the 37th Annual Meeting of the Association for Computational Linguistics*, pages 505–512, College Park, Maryland, USA, June. Association for Computational Linguistics.

Devlin, J., Chang, M.-W., Lee, K., and Toutanova, K. (2019). BERT: Pre-training of deep bidirectional transformers for language understanding. In *Proceedings of the 2019 Conference of the North American Chapter of the Association for Computational Linguistics: Human Language Technologies, Volume 1 (Long and Short Papers)*, pages 4171–4186, Minneapolis, Minnesota, June. Association for Computational Linguistics.

Di Sciullo, A.-M., Muysken, P., and Singh, R. (1986). Government and code-mixing. *Journal of linguistics*, 22(1):1–24.

Durrett, G. and Klein, D. (2015). Neural CRF parsing. In *Proceedings of the 53rd Annual Meeting of the Association for Computational Linguistics and the 7th International Joint Conference on Natural Language Processing (Volume 1: Long Papers)*, pages 302–312, Beijing, China, July. Association for Computational Linguistics.

Dyer, C., Kuncoro, A., Ballesteros, M., and Smith, N. A. (2016). Recurrent neural network grammars. In *Proceedings of the 2016 Conference of the North American Chapter of the Association for Computational Linguistics: Human Language Technologies*, pages 199–209, San Diego, California, June. Association for Computational Linguistics.

Finkel, J. R., Kleeman, A., and Manning, C. D. (2008). Efficient, feature-based, conditional random field parsing. In *Proceedings of ACL-08: HLT*, pages 959–967, Columbus, Ohio, June. Association for Computational Linguistics.

Joshi, A. K. (1982). Processing of sentences with intra-sentential code-switching. In *Coling 1982: Proceedings of the Ninth International Conference on Computational Linguistics*.

Kitaev, N. and Klein, D. (2018). Constituency parsing with a self-attentive encoder. In *Proceedings of the 56th Annual Meeting of the Association for Computational Linguistics (Volume 1: Long Papers)*, pages 2676–2686, Melbourne, Australia, July. Association for Computational Linguistics.

Klein, D. and Manning, C. D. (2003). Accurate unlexicalized parsing. In *Proceedings of the 41st Annual Meeting of the Association for Computational Linguistics*, pages 423–430, Sapporo, Japan, July. Association for Computational Linguistics.

Kunchukuttan, A., Mehta, P., and Bhattacharyya, P. (2018). The IIT Bombay English-Hindi parallel corpus. In *Proceedings of the Eleventh International Conference on Language Resources and Evaluation (LREC 2018)*, Miyazaki, Japan, May. European Language Resources Association (ELRA).

Lee, Y.-S. and Wang, Z. (2016). Language independent dependency to constituent tree conversion. In *Proceedings of COLING 2016, the 26th International Conference on Computational Linguistics: Technical Papers*, pages 421–428, Osaka, Japan, December. The COLING 2016 Organizing Committee.

Milroy, J. (1995). *One speaker, two languages: Cross-disciplinary perspectives on code-switching*. Cambridge University Press.

Partanen, N., Lim, K., Rießler, M., and Poibeau, T. (2018). Dependency parsing of code-switching data with cross-lingual feature representations. In *Proceedings of the Fourth International Workshop on Computational Linguistics of Uralic Languages*, pages 1–17, Helsinki, Finland, January. Association for Computational Linguistics.

Poplack, S. (1980). Sometimes i'll start a sentence in spanish y termino en espanol: toward a typology of code-switching1. *Linguistics*, 18(7-8):581–618.

Pratapa, A., Bhat, G., Choudhury, M., Sitaram, S., Dandapat, S., and Bali, K. (2018). Language modeling for code-mixing: The role of linguistic theory based synthetic data. In *Proceedings of the 56th Annual Meeting of the Association for Computational Linguistics (Volume 1: Long Papers)*, pages 1543–1553, Melbourne, Australia, July. Association for Computational Linguistics.

Rijhwani, S., Sequiera, R., Choudhury, M., Bali, K., and Maddila, C. S. (2017). Estimating code-switching on twitter with a novel generalized word-level language detection technique. In *Proceedings of the 55th Annual Meeting of the Association for Computational Linguistics (Volume 1: Long Papers)*, pages 1971–1982, Vancouver, Canada, July. Association for Computational Linguistics.

Sankoff, D. (1998). The production of code-mixed discourse. In *Proceedings of the 17th international conference on Computational linguistics-Volume 1*, pages 8–21. Association for Computational Linguistics.

Sequiera, R., Choudhury, M., Gupta, P., Rosso, P., Kumar, S., Banerjee, S., Naskar, S. K., Bandyopadhyay, S., Chittaranjan, G., Das, A., et al. (2015). Overview of fire-2015 shared task on mixed script information retrieval.

Solorio, T., Blair, E., Maharjan, S., Bethard, S., Diab, M., Ghoneim, M., Hawwari, A., AlGhamdi, F., Hirschberg, J., Chang, A., and Fung, P. (2014). Overview for the first shared task on language identification in code-switched data. In *Proceedings of the First Workshop on Computational Approaches to Code Switching*, pages 62–72, Doha, Qatar, October. Association for Computational Linguistics.

Stern, M., Andreas, J., and Klein, D. (2017). A minimal span-based neural constituency parser. In *Proceedings of the 55th Annual Meeting of the Association for Computational Linguistics (Volume 1: Long Papers)*, pages 818–827, Vancouver, Canada, July. Association for Computational Linguistics.

Thang, L. Q., Noji, H., and Miyao, Y. (2015). Optimal shift-reduce constituent parsing with structured perceptron. In *Proceedings of the 53rd Annual Meeting of the Association for Computational Linguistics and the 7th International Joint Conference on Natural Language Processing (Volume 1: Long Papers)*, pages 1534–1544, Beijing, China, July. Association for Computational Linguistics.

Vinyals, O., Kaiser, Ł., Koo, T., Petrov, S., Sutskever, I., and Hinton, G. (2015). Grammar as a foreign language. In *Advances in neural information processing systems*, pages 2773–2781.

Vyas, Y., Gella, S., Sharma, J., Bali, K., and Choudhury, M. (2014). POS tagging of English-Hindi code-mixed social media content. In *Proceedings of the 2014 Conference on Empirical Methods in Natural Language Processing (EMNLP)*, pages 974–979, Doha, Qatar, October. Association for Computational Linguistics.

Wang, Z. and Zong, C. (2010). Phrase structure parsing with dependency structure. In *Coling 2010: Posters*, pages 1292–1300, Beijing, China, August. Coling 2010 Organizing Committee.

Xia, F. and Palmer, M. (2001). Converting dependency structures to phrase structures. In *Proceedings of the First International Conference on Human Language Technology Research*.

Xia, F., Rambow, O., Bhatt, R., Palmer, M., and Misra Sharma, D. (2008). Towards a multi-representational treebank. *LOT Occasional Series*, 12:159–170.

Younger, D. H. (1967). Recognition and parsing of context-free languages in time n3. *Information and control*, 10(2):189–208.

A. Error Analysis on Trees

Depicted below are 3 trees from Real Test and the parser's prediction for these trees. Gold trees are on the left and the parser's predictions are on the right. Errors made by the parser and possible reasons for the same have been mentioned along with the trees. The parsing F1 score for each tree is also reported, and the trees are ordered in descending order of this score.

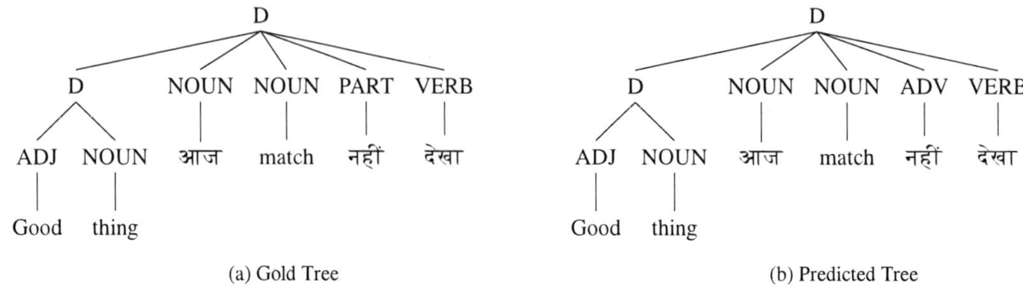

(a) Gold Tree   (b) Predicted Tree

Figure 4: **F1: 100.0**: The parser predicts one of the POS tags incorrectly, but otherwise predicts the tree structure correctly.

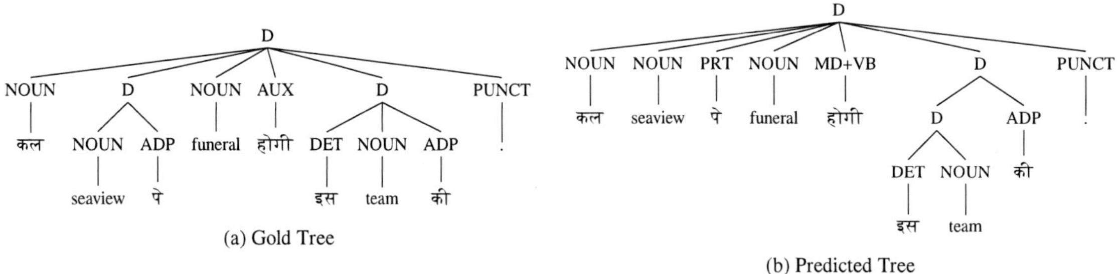

(a) Gold Tree

(b) Predicted Tree

Figure 5: **F1: 66.67**: The parser predicts the POS tag for पे incorrectly, leading to the subtree (D → NOUN ADP) not being captured properly.

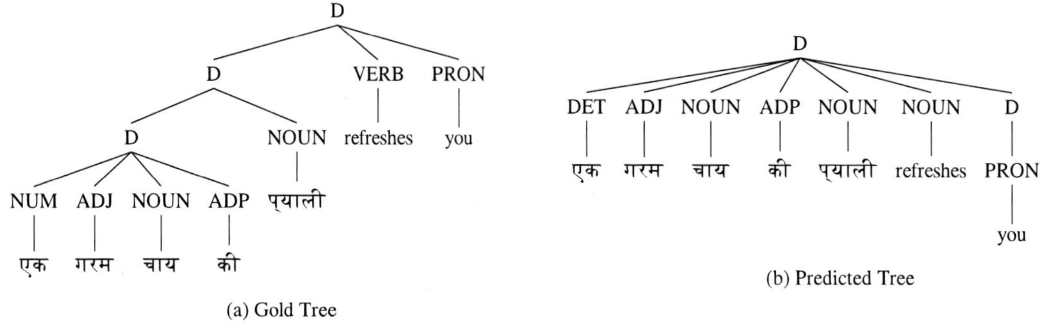

(a) Gold Tree

(b) Predicted Tree

Figure 6: **F1: 40.0**: There are a few POS tag errors in this case. As sentences get longer, the parser struggles to capture the tree structure of the original sentence and outputs a tree where the root node derives (almost) all the leaf nodes directly.

Proceedings of the LREC 2020 – 4th Workshop on Computational Approaches to Code Switching, pages 65–70
Language Resources and Evaluation Conference (LREC 2020), Marseille, 11–16 May 2020
European Language Resources Association (ELRA), licensed under CC-BY-NC

Towards an Efficient Code-Mixed Grapheme-to-Phoneme Conversion in an Agglutinative Language: A Case Study on To-Korean Transliteration

Won Ik Cho, Seok Min Kim, Nam Soo Kim
Department of Electrical and Computer Engineering and INMC, Seoul National University,
wicho@hi.snu.ac.kr, smkim@hi.snu.ac.kr, nkim@snu.ac.kr

Abstract

Code-mixed grapheme-to-phoneme (G2P) conversion is a crucial issue for modern speech recognition and synthesis task, but has been seldom investigated in sentence-level in literature. In this study, we construct a system that performs precise and efficient multi-stage code-mixed G2P conversion, for a less studied agglutinative language, Korean. The proposed system undertakes a sentence-level transliteration that is effective in the accurate processing of Korean text. We formulate the underlying philosophy that supports our approach and demonstrate how it fits with the contemporary document.

Keywords: code-mixed G2P, sentence-level transliteration, agglutinative language, open-source software

1. Introduction

Grapheme-to-phoneme (G2P) conversion is an essential process for speech recognition and synthesis. It converts textual information called *grapheme* into phonetic information called *phoneme*. The graphemes, represented by symbols that let the language users pronounce, are not real audio data, nor do not have a necessary correspondence with the genuine sound. For example, 'apple' sounds more like *æpl*, while 'America' sounds like *əmérikə*. This process implies that the character 'a' does not have a direct correspondence with the sound 'æ' or 'ə'; instead, the appropriate symbol to transcribe each pronunciation might have been 'a'. This is influenced by that the English alphabet is a segmental script, but other writing systems do not necessarily guarantee greater correspondence. For example, in the case of logograms such as Chinese characters, there is little relationship between the composition of the character (*bushu*) and the pronunciation of the symbol (Figure 1, top).

In a little different viewpoint notwithstanding, Hangul representation of Korean is a featural writing system (Daniels and Bright, 1996) in which each sub-characters of morphosyllabic blocks corresponds to a phonetic property (Figure 1, bottom) (Kim-Renaud, 1997). For instance, in a syllable *khak* placed at the right end of the bottom of Figure 1, the three clock-wisely arranged characters *kh*, *a*, and *k*, which sound *khiukh* (among 19 candidates), *ah* (among 21 candidates), and *kiyek* (among 27 candidates), refers to the *first*, the *second* and the *third* sound of the given character, respectively (Cho et al., 2019). This is a unique feature of the Korean writing system, which distinguishes Hangul from Chinese characters that do not have a direct relationship with syllable pronunciations. Also, Hangul is more delicately decomposed compared to mora-level Japanese Kana.

Due to the above characteristics, the process of transforming grapheme in Korean to phoneme is widely performed by using the Korean alphabet itself (Jeon et al., 1998; Kim et al., 2002), that is, the Hangul sub-character *Jamo*, unlike cases such as Chinese *pinyin* that borrows the English alphabet (Figure 1, top). For this reason, even though the widely used Korean G2P sometimes uses English expressions (Cho, 2017), the full phoneme sequence is primarily

Figure 1: Comparing the Chinese language written with Hanzi (along with *pinyin*, top) and the Korean language written with Hangul, the featural writing system (along with Yale romanization, bottom).

written in Hangul Jamo, to reflect the Korean pronunciation system. This property, the grapheme and phoneme set sharing the same symbols, allows Korean G2P a phonological approach within the language itself.

Currently, Korean G2P systems in use (Cho, 2017; Park, 2019) follow the pronunciation rules of the National Institute of Korean Language in principle, and we can confirm that the conventional modules perform well on a rule-based basis. However, in this study, we implement a preprocessing module for challenging code-mixed G2P, which regards co-existing Korean and non-Korean expressions (Shim, 1994), considering the case where the basis cannot be found in the monolingual rule. In specific, we deal with the English alphabet and Chinese characters, and mainly on the former[1], concerning that environment in which English is mixed with text often exist in modern scripts such as technical reports or scripts (Shim, 1994; Sitaram et al., 2019).

---

[1]Depending on the configuration and arrangement of Chinese characters, the duration of the syllable may change or a particular consonant may be inserted, but this is a task to handle in G2P after converting to a Hangul once and not a target here. Also, Japanese Kana is seldom used among Korean text.

Due to the human language being arbitrary, there are limitations in obtaining phoneme sequences using only the rules in some cases. Firstly, because code-mixing is not restricted only to two languages (ko-en), that English letters co-existing with Chinese characters and numbers are also observable. Second, various acronyms with non-deterministic pronunciation exist and are frequently utilized (e.g., word2vec, G2P), usually not spoken in a code-switched way. Finally, due to the agglutinative property of the Korean language, it is often vague to decide which phrase to transform within a sentence. Accordingly, we decided to fully utilize the information given by existing libraries and dictionaries to implement a sentence-level transliteration for Korean/English code-mixed G2P, taking into account the syntactic property of decomposed tokens. The contributions of this study and demonstration are as follows:

- Easily adjustable multi-stage system for a sentence-level code-mixed Korean G2P; detecting foreign expressions and replacing them with Hangul terms

- Suggesting morphological and phonological tricks that can handle the pronunciation of cumbersome non-Korean expressions

The system and code is to be publicly available[2].

2.   Background

Sentence-level transliteration may seem simple, but it is involved in all phonetics, phonology, and morphology. In other words, at least the background in the Korean writing system, morphological analysis, Korean-English code-mixed writing is essential for implementing en-ko code-switching G2P (Kim et al., 2002). Phonetically, the Korean language is a language pronounced as a sequence of syllables, and the related phonemes locally correspond to graphemes represented by morpho-syllabic blocks (Kim-Renaud, 1997). The grapheme consists of a block as a single character, and is decomposed to sub-characters of first to third sound; CV(C). They are spoken straightforwardly in singleton cases, but when two or more characters are contiguous, the pronunciation differs from that of the single one (Jeon et al., 1998).

A code-mixed sentence, in this paper, is a Korean utterance (mainly written in text), where the syntax follows the Korean grammar, but some content phrases (non-functional expressions) are replaced by non-Korean terms, including English, Chinese and some numbers (Figure 2) (Shim, 1994). These expressions are often not promising in pronunciation for users of the same language, and acronyms are often confusing to resolve even when the source language is known (e.g., LREC as el-rec, or AAAI as triple-A-I). Therefore, for G2P, the biggest problem that code-mixed sentences bring is the difficulty of applying a rule for generating a phoneme sequence for speech processing, especially speech synthesis (Chandu et al., 2017). This, in turn, is directly related to the difficulty of transliteration (Sitaram et al., 2019).

---

[2]https://github.com/warnikchow/translit2k

G2P의 관점에서, code-mixed 文章이 가져오는 가장 큰 문제점은, 音聲 처리, 특히 音聲 합성에 文章을 活用하는 데에 있어, 기존의 음소 sequence를 생성하는 rule을 적용하기 어렵다는 것이다.

Figure 2: Given that the modern Korean writing system does not utilize Chinese characters, the sentence above is a code-mixed Korean sentence with Chinese characters (green), English words (blue), and numbers (yellow). The translation is: *"From the point of view of G2P, the biggest problem with code-mixed text is that it is difficult to apply the rules for generating existing phonetic sequences in the use of text for speech processing, especially for speech synthesis."*

There has been a lot of work on word-level transliteration process and its evaluation (Kang and Kim, 2000; Oh and Choi, 2002; Oh and Choi, 2005; Oh et al., 2006), but little on the sentence-level processings. Unlike in English, where each word consists of either source or target language that arbitrary word can be transliterated into the source language, In Korean code-mixed sentences, it is usual that the foreign expressions are augmented with the functional particles, in a truly code-mixed format in morphological level (Figure 2). It looks like a pidgin language, but is fully comprehensible by native readers since the symbols are distinguished. It is assumed that many industrial units are applying various heuristics to handle them, but we could not find an established academic approach for this issue. Built on the preceding discussions on code-mixed sentences and transliteration, we provide a detailed description of our resolution afterward.

3.   Proposed Method

As the main contribution of this paper, we will implement a sentence-level code-mixed G2P that operates efficiently. For this, we took two methods into account.

(1) On training a transformation module that maps Korean/non-Korean code-mixed raw text directly to Korean phoneme sequence

(2) Multi-stage method of primarily changing non-Korean vocabulary to Korean pronunciation in code-mixed text and applying separate G2P module

The method of (1) is very suitable for utilizing neural network-based training and the implementation of end-to-end speech recognition/synthesis system, but usually, the number of Korean lexicons is significantly higher than the English vocabulary size. In other words, as long as Korean sentences are used for speech recognition or synthesis, a large amount of artificially made code-mixed sentences are required for reliable learning, of which the effectiveness is not guaranteed. In addition, it does not seem data-efficient in that Korean text dominant in the dataset may deter the enhancement of transliterating arbitrary foreign expressions. These issues can result in the degradation of G2P precision and the performance of recognition/synthesis.

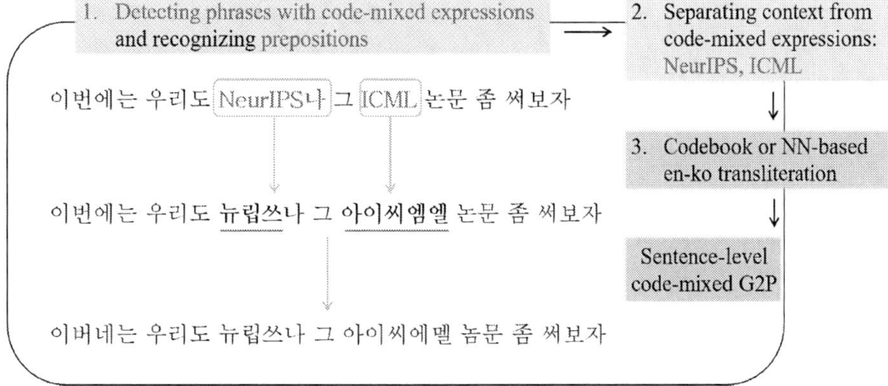

Figure 3: A brief diagram of the proposed code-mixed transliteration system. The translation is: *"Why don't we write a NeurIPS or ICML paper this year?"*, and the non-Korean terms *NeurIPS* and *ICML* are identified and transformed.

On the other hand, in (2), non-Korean expressions are transliterated into Korean primarily, and then rule-based precise Korean G2P is performed. For the latter part of the process, a well-used module already exists (Cho, 2017; Park, 2019), so we can concentrate on performing the former task, the transliteration to Korean. In this study, we adopt (2), mainly enhancing the transliteration process by detecting English and other non-Korean expressions (including Chinese characters and numbers) in code-mixed sentences and transforming them into Korean pronunciation. The specific procedure using the method of (2) is as Following (Figure 3).

1. **Detecting phrases with code-mixed expressions:** First of all, in the result of merely splitting a sentence into white space, detect an eojeol (Korean term for a whitespace-split word) containing an English or non-Korean (Chinese characters, numbers) expressions. In this process, Unicode information is exploited. The tokenization is done basically by a morphological analyzer, and each eojeol is considered as a chunk of morphemes.

2. **Separating context:** Subsequently, use the eojeols of interest as the target of transformation, except for the functional particles (if present). In this process, the outcome of the morphological analyzer above is adopted.

3. **Hybrid transliteration:** Finally, transliterate the detected English/non-Korean expressions into Korean pronunciation. It is viable to use a dictionary or train a neural network-based model, but we want to mix the two approaches. In more detail, one can collect a variety of English loanwords, and list them with the commonly used (lexicographical) Korean pronunciations, using it as a dictionary. After the primary rule-based transliteration, a trained transliteration system can be used for words that do not fall into the pre-defined categories. In this process, Chinese characters and numbers are all taken into account, along with the context that is present in the rest of eojeol. The tricks used here are:

- Trick 1. **On Chinese characters:** All Chinese characters are replaced with corresponding Hangul symbols, since such cases are Sino-Koreans which already

have an established pronunciation. Here, a subsequent chunk of Chinese characters is tied and transformed together to reflect the possible change of pronunciation regarding word-initial rules. If the Chinese character and numbers/English alphabet come together, the Chinese characters are transformed first, followed by the transliteration of other parts.

- Trick 2. **On numbers:** For lone case, the pronunciation may follow the corresponding Chinese character as default, and if not alone, the tokens nearby are taken into account. If a number is placed between English words, consider using the result of transliteration of English words into Korean (e.g., 2 = two > *thu*, 4 = four > *pho*). Even when a number is between the English alphabet and Chinese/Korean at the same time, the pronunciation may follow English, as in the case of '*number 3 kka-ci* (till number 3)'. Otherwise, between Chinese characters, the number is read as in Trick 1. If the number between is followed by Korean Hangul, the cardinality, ordinality, or being Sino-Korean of the number is determined upon a convention, which might change the pronunciation. This follows the conventions of the Korean language, and can be modified based on the dictionary.

- Trick 3. **On acronyms:** Acronyms are easy to detect if written in capital letters, but people do not necessarily follow such the standard. Therefore, we added some tricks for the ones that are not in the dictionary. If they are all composed of consonants or have separate symbols between characters, each consonant is subsequently pronounced in Korean. However, if there is a corresponding English word, the dictionary output, or the result that is yielded by the trained system is used.

In the above process, methods such as a recurrent neural network (RNN) or Transformer (Vaswani et al., 2017) may be used for machine learning approach through training. The method using training means to make seq2seq (Sutskever et al., 2014) model with alphabet input and Hangul output using a parallel corpus of English and transliterated English. However, it is not necessary to take a training-based approach to English words that are already in the dictionary. Thus, words in the codebook[3] produce a precise output in the form of look-up tables, and words not in the codebook are predicted by seq2seq models learned through parallel corpus (here it is the same as the codebook). This allows the model to learn pronunciations for words that are not in the dictionary, and possibly for acronyms, as many previous machine learning-based transliteration modules did (Karimi et al., 2011; Finch et al., 2016). Translating English into Korean first in this way and then applying rule-based G2P allows the modeling of the entire G2P to be more robust to Korean pronunciation rules.

We note here that though the codebook we adopt already incorporates a precise transformation of many words (about 37K), we need to train a system that can pronounce words that are not on the list. That is, we need to observe beyond the rules of how the arrangement of English consonants and vowels has determined Korean pronunciation. Once the Hangul characters are padded sub-character-level, or jamo-level, and compared with the English alphabet, the correspondence between the two is not consistent. Beyond the limitation of symbol representation, what makes this more challenging are 1) the different sound produced by the Korean consonants that come to the first and third sound, and 2) the sound change that takes place when the third sound meets the first sound of the next syllable. Moreover, 3) in English, one needs to observe the vowels where the consonant is located around, the vowel placement within the word, and what unique phonetic properties the various bigram/trigram characters have.

Therefore, in the implementation of a non-rule-based transliteration system, the seq2seq approach is carried out to character level in English and sub-character-level in Korean. Moreover, in characterizing Korean, the first sound and the third sound, that are similarly the consonant, can be represented distinctly. Using this, with about 37K pairs of English word-Korean pronunciation pairs, we trained the (attention-based) RNN encoder-decoder (Cho et al., 2014; Luong et al., 2015), under the consideration that the Transformer would be too large-scale for just a word-level transformation. The implementation detail is to be released along with the model and system.

4. Experiment

The concept of sentence-level code-mixed Korean G2P has been proposed in the previous section, and we aim to implement a fast and accurate code-mixed G2P that can be used for practical speech recognition/synthesis, that integrates other models in use. However, since standard transliteration studies have sought for character/word-level accuracy, mainly in word-level transformations, referring them might not be suitable for direct comparison with this work. Therefore, in this section, we will demonstrate the flexibility and utility of our approach with a concrete example.

4.1. Implementation

For an efficient construction that divides and conquers the sub-modules, we leveraged various open-source libraries in our implementation. The sub-modules and corresponding libraries are as follows:

- **mixed_g2p:** Transforms a code-mixed sentence to the phoneme sequence. Consists of *sentranslit* and *KoG2P/g2pK*.
    - *KoG2P[4]:* An easily employable Python-based Korean G2P library that transforms the Korean text to alphabetical symbols that represent the Korean phonemes, based on a rulebook.
    - *g2pK[5]:* An up-to-date Python-based open-source G2P library for Korean, that transforms a Korean grapheme sequence to a Hangul syllable sequence that is more familiar with human reading.

- **sentranslit:** Performs sentence-level transliteration of code-mixed sentences. Consists of *align_particles*, *trans_eojeol* (eojeol-level transliteration), *trans_number*, *trans_hanja*, and *trans_latin*. Undertakes transliteration only if the string contains non-Hangul expressions.
    - *hgtk[6]:* A software that recognizes, decomposes, and reconstructs Hangul/Jamo sequence. Also detects if the string contains Chinese characters or the Latin alphabet.

- **trans_eojeol:** Controls the operation of *trans_number*, *trans_hanja*, and *trans_latin*, given the result of morphological analysis.
    - *MeCab[7]:* A statistic model-based Korean morphological analyzer that performs fast and accurate, which was first developed for the analysis of the Japanese language. Here, we utilize *python-mecab[8]* for convenience, which is an easily accessible wrapper.

- **trans_number:** Reads the numbers in Chinese style (Korean pronunciation), in English (en-ko transliteration), or in Korean (ordinal, cardinal, or Sino-Korean).
    - Bases on the characteristics of the context tokens, incorporating various exceptional cases.

- **trans_hanja:** Reads Chinese characters in Korean pronunciation, considering the word-initial rules.
    - *hanja[9]:* A library that translates Chinese characters into Korean syllables, also obeying word-initial rules. This module is utilized in two parts of the system; at the very first of the sentence analysis and again in eojeol-level, to complement the possible fail of Chinese character recognition.

- **trans_latin:** Performs en-ko transliteration, with rule and learning hybrid approach.

---

[3]In this paper, we interchangeably utilize *codebook* and *dictionary*.

[4]https://github.com/scarletcho/KoG2P
[5]https://github.com/Kyubyong/g2pK
[6]https://github.com/bluedisk/hangul-toolkit
[7]https://bitbucket.org/eunjeon/mecab-ko-dic/src/master/
[8]https://github.com/jeongukjae/python-mecab
[9]https://github.com/suminb/hanja

```
>>> from sentranslit import sentranslit as trans

>>> trans('G2P의 관점에서, code-mix 文章이 가져오
는 가장 큰 문제점은, 音聲 처리, 특히 音聲 합성에 文章
을 活用하는 데에 있어, 기존의 음소 sequence를 생성하
는 rule을 적용하기 어렵다는 것이다.')

'지투피의 관점에서, 코드-믹스 문장이 가져오는 가장 큰
문제점은, 음성 처리, 특히 음성 합성에 문장을 활용하는 데
에 있어, 기존의 음소 시퀀스를 생성하는 룰을 적용하기 어
렵다는 것이다.'
```

Figure 4: Demonstration for the sample sentence in Figure 2. Note that the code-mixed expressions in each eojeol are transliterated based on the scheme and tricks in Section 3.

- *transliteration*[10]: Our utilized dictionary comes from the pre-built dataset[11] of this library, where the results of learning-based en-ko transliteration was previously published. We train a new system based on this, and this module can be replaced with whatever transliteration module that shows sufficient performance.

4.2. Demonstration

Our demonstration with the sample sentence in Figure 2 is suggested in Figure 4. Since the G2P conversion is straight-forwardly performed, we discuss here the sentence-level transliteration process.

There are mainly three points that show how our system works. First, regarding Chinese code-mixed expressions, some in sole words and others mixed with Korean functional particles, our module (*trans_eojeol*) detects the terms and translate them into Korean pronunciation via *trans_hanja*, with the help of *hanja* library. Next, similar is done for English expressions such as *code*, *mix*, *sequence* and *rule*, possibly utilizing *trans_latin*, where the dictionary and training are engaged in. Lastly, for a challenging term *G2P*, which may not be in the dictionary (and is at the first place decomposed by the morphological analyzer), the sub-modules above succeed to split them into G, 2, and P, transliterating each of them to Korean pronunciation *ci*, *thu*, and *phi*, given that g and p should be read as a single alphabet (due to being sole consonant) and also 2 is read in English concerning its surroundings. In this way, our module divides and conquers the challenging task and finally yields the desired output.

4.3. Discussion

Though our work is mainly on a code-mixed G2P, the recently released library *g2pK* partially shares some features with ours; various functions are inserted regarding the pronunciation of English terms and numbers in Korean sentences. We concentrate more on reading numbers and acronyms in a code-mixed context, trying to make a rule-learning hybrid approach for en-ko transliteration. On the other hand, in *g2pK*, such functions are implemented as a utility, while G2P rules are main and quite thoroughly investigated. We claim that both systems are not mutually exclusive, and rather might be complementary to each other. Again, to be specific on the architecture, each of our sub-modules can be replaced with whatever the user wants as customization, without losing the additional flexibility of the user-generated dictionary. For instance, as suggested in *transliteration* library, one can define a new word list and accumulate the wanted result to it. Making up a look-up table can sometimes and inevitably be more efficient and accurate. Also, since MeCab was basically proposed for the analysis of the Japanese language, whose syntax a lot resembles Korean, one who wants to implement a similar module for Japanese code-mixed writings may benefit our system. The above factors support the scalability and generalizability of our approach.

5. Application

The code-mixed G2P implemented in this paper can be used for both research and industry. First of all, as emphasized, the application onto speech synthesis is very intuitive. Korean corpus has many sentences that consist only of Hangul characters, of course, but there may also be enough code-mixed expressions in modern text, and especially in chat dialogues, which is close to being synthesized. Therefore, if one can take advantage of this system well, it might be possible to promote plausible code-mixed pronunciation without regulating the generation of the script to only one kind of language. Without a doubt, this does not have a conflict with the option of not doing code-switching. That is, merely preserving the pronunciation of the source language is also recommended, if technically available.

The multi-stage approach we present can, of course, generate bottlenecks. However, it is expected to have significant advantages over end-to-end learning, in other words, using code-mixed text for training speech synthesis systems. For instance, the English language, once used with Korean notation, hardly reflects the phonetic traits shared with other Korean alphabets. This is primarily because the structure of CV(C) is not clear in the English writing system as in Hangul. Also, since agglutinative language usually displays functional particles after nouns or verbs, a corpus configuration with insufficient English words does not guarantee the performance of end-to-end architecture. It is also challenging to ensure that doing so yields transliterated pronunciations that we pronounce in real life, nor better than the transliteration modules that concentrate on word-level seq2seq. Therefore, we believe that it is practically advantageous to detect non-Korean expressions first and use hybrid transformation with some tricks.

The implementation of G2P for speech synthesis is a typical application, but besides, this algorithm can be exploited in sentence correction, corpus refinement, script construction/pronunciation guidelines, and translation service quality improvement. Also, this methodology is expected to apply not only to Chinese characters, English words, and numbers in Korean sentences, but also to sentences and code-mixed expressions in various agglutinative languages, especially the ones that require morphological analysis.

---

[10]https://github.com/muik/transliteration

[11]https://github.com/muik/transliteration/tree/master/data/source

6. Conclusion

In this paper, we constructed a stable and efficient g2p by presenting a hybrid transliteration method with rule and training for code-mixed Korean sentences. To this end, we detected words containing non-Korean expressions, separated a grammatical part of the word from the rest content via morphological analysis, and replaced the code-mixed expressions with transliterated ones.

In this process, by using a statistical model-based morphological analyzer with fairly high performance, we performed non-Korean expression detection that is suitable for colloquial context, with a less computational burden. Also, by separating the grammatical part from the content part in this process, the actual part that needs to be converted in the code-mixed sentence is detected so that the expressions that contain English/Chinese/number can be smoothly converted into Korean pronunciation.

Our subsequent studies aim to improve the accuracy of handling proper nouns in code-mixed text pre-processing by collecting more commercial expressions. Also, we plan to verify common pronunciation patterns through media/real-life examples, exploiting the neural network structure with external memory. As a result, research will be carried out to enable controllable to-Korean transliteration by allowing more user-specified stop-words to be reflected in the training of the systems and conversion process itself.

7. Acknowledgements

This research was supported by Projects for Research and Development of Police science and Technology under Center for Research and Development of Police science and Technology and Korean National Police Agency funded by the Ministry of Science, ICT and Future Planning (PA-J000001-2017-101). Also, this work was supported by the Technology Innovation Program (10076583, Development of free-running speech recognition technologies for embedded robot system) funded By the Ministry of Trade, Industry & Energy (MOTIE, Korea). Besides, we thank to the three anonymous reviewers for their helpful comments. After all, the authors appreciate all the contributors of the open source libraries which were essential for our project.

8. Bibliographical References

Chandu, K. R., Rallabandi, S. K., Sitaram, S., and Black, A. W. (2017). Speech synthesis for mixed-language navigation instructions. In *INTERSPEECH*, pages 57–61.

Cho, K., Van Merriënboer, B., Gulcehre, C., Bahdanau, D., Bougares, F., Schwenk, H., and Bengio, Y. (2014). Learning phrase representations using rnn encoder-decoder for statistical machine translation. *arXiv preprint arXiv:1406.1078*.

Cho, W. I., Kim, S. M., and Kim, N. S. (2019). Investigating an effective character-level embedding in Korean sentence classification. *arXiv preprint arXiv:1905.13656*.

Cho, Y. (2017). Korean grapheme-to-phoneme analyzer (kog2p). https://github.com/scarletcho/KoG2P.

Daniels, P. T. and Bright, W. (1996). *The world's writing systems*. Oxford University Press on Demand.

Finch, A., Liu, L., Wang, X., and Sumita, E. (2016). Target-bidirectional neural models for machine transliteration. In *Proceedings of the sixth named entity workshop*, pages 78–82.

Jeon, J., Cha, S., Chung, M., Park, J., and Hwang, K. (1998). Automatic generation of Korean pronunciation variants by multistage applications of phonological rules. In *Fifth International Conference on Spoken Language Processing*.

Kang, I.-H. and Kim, G. (2000). English-to-Korean transliteration using multiple unbounded overlapping phoneme chunks. In *Proceedings of the 18th conference on Computational linguistics-Volume 1*, pages 418–424. Association for Computational Linguistics.

Karimi, S., Scholer, F., and Turpin, A. (2011). Machine transliteration survey. *ACM Computing Surveys (CSUR)*, 43(3):1–46.

Kim, B., Lee, G. G., and Lee, J.-H. (2002). Morpheme-based grapheme to phoneme conversion using phonetic patterns and morphophonemic connectivity information. *ACM Transactions on Asian Language Information Processing (TALIP)*, 1(1):65–82.

Kim-Renaud, Y.-K. (1997). The phonological analysis reflected in the Korean writing system. *The Korean alphabet: its history and structure*, pages 161–192.

Luong, M.-T., Pham, H., and Manning, C. D. (2015). Effective approaches to attention-based neural machine translation. *arXiv preprint arXiv:1508.04025*.

Oh, J.-H. and Choi, K.-S. (2002). An English-Korean transliteration model using pronunciation and contextual rules. In *Proceedings of the 19th international conference on Computational linguistics-Volume 1*, pages 1–7. Association for Computational Linguistics.

Oh, J.-H. and Choi, K.-S. (2005). An ensemble of grapheme and phoneme for machine transliteration. In *International Conference on Natural Language Processing*, pages 450–461. Springer.

Oh, J., Choi, K., and Isahara, H. (2006). A comparison of different machine transliteration models. *Journal of Artificial Intelligence Research*, 27:119–151.

Park, K. (2019). g2pk. https://github.com/Kyubyong/g2pk.

Shim, R. J. (1994). Englishized Korean: Structure, status, and attitudes. *World Englishes*, 13(2):225–244.

Sitaram, S., Chandu, K. R., Rallabandi, S. K., and Black, A. W. (2019). A survey of code-switched speech and language processing. *arXiv preprint arXiv:1904.00784*.

Sutskever, I., Vinyals, O., and Le, Q. V. (2014). Sequence to sequence learning with neural networks. In *Advances in neural information processing systems*, pages 3104–3112.

Vaswani, A., Shazeer, N., Parmar, N., Uszkoreit, J., Jones, L., Gomez, A. N., Kaiser, Ł., and Polosukhin, I. (2017). Attention is all you need. In *Advances in Neural Information Processing Systems*, pages 5998–6008.

Association for Computational Linguistics
209 N. Eighth Street
Stroudsburg, Pennsylvania 18360

ISBN 978-1-7138-1258-6